DREAMS IN WHITE

DUNCAN GRAHAM

CURRENCY PRESS
SYDNEY

GRIFFIN
THE COMPANY
SYDNEY

CURRENCY PLAYS

First published in 2013
by Currency Press Pty Ltd,
PO Box 2287, Strawberry Hills, NSW, 2012, Australia
enquiries@currency.com.au
www.currency.com.au
in association with Griffin Theatre Company

National Library of Australia CIP data is available from the National Library of
Australia Catalogue: http://catalogue.nla.gov.au

Typeset by Dean Nottle for Currency Press.
Cover photograph by Katie Kaars. Cover design by Interbrand.
Front cover shows Andrew MacFarlane and Lucy Bell.

Currency Press acknowledges the Traditional Owners of the Country on which
we live and work. We pay our respects to all Aboriginal and Torres Strait
Islander Elders, past and present.

Contents

To Graeme Fife: godfather and friend:

Homo sum, humani nihil a me alienum puto
[I am a human being, I consider nothing that is human alien to me]

Terrence (195/185–159 BC)

Dreams in White was first produced by the Griffin Theatre Company at SBW Stables Theatre, Sydney, on 8 February 2013, with the following cast:

ANNE DEVINE / JULIA WHITE	LUCY BELL
PAULA ANDERSON / PSYCHIATRIST	MANDY McELHINNEY
MICHAEL DEVINE / RAY WIMPLE	ANDREW McFARLANE
DAVID WHITE / GARY ANDERSON / DETECTIVE McNAUGHT	STEVE RODGERS
AMY DEVINE	SARA WEST

Director, Tanya Goldberg
Dramaturg, Tessa Leong
Designer, Teresa Negroponte
Lighting Designer, Hartley T A Kemp
Composer, Kelly Ryall

CHARACTERS

The play should be performed by five actors, as follows:

ACTOR 1, 50

MICHAEL DEVINE, property developer

RAY WIMPLE, landscaper

ACTOR 2, 40s

ANNE DEVINE, wife of Michael Devine

JULIA WHITE, prospective buyer

ACTOR 3, 18

AMY DEVINE, Michael and Anne's daughter

ACTOR 4, 40s

DAVID WHITE, husband of prospective buyer

GARY ANDERSON, unemployed

DETECTIVE McNAUGHT, investigating the case of Michael Devine's disappearance

ACTOR 5, 40s

PAULA ANDERSON, wife of Gary

PSYCHIATRIST, treating Anne Devine

VOICE

SETTING

All action takes place in one living room.

NOTE

Time for each scene is indicated in the script as *before* or *after*—referring to Michael Devine's disappearance. This should not be indicated in the production.

This play went to press before the end of rehearsals and may differ from the play as performed.

1. FIVE MINUTES BEFORE

GARY *and* PAULA.

PAULA: There's so much shit out there, there's not enough room to swing a cat.

GARY: Why do you wanta swing a cat?

PAULA: Don't start with me.

GARY: I'm not starting.

PAULA: What're you gonna do, Gary?

GARY: When?

PAULA: When you clean up the wrecking yard out there. I can't even get to the bloody line.

GARY: Concrete.

PAULA: Concrete?

GARY: Yep. With Mitch.

PAULA: Concrete with Mitch?

GARY: Yep, he's offered me one of his trucks. He's killin' it. Makes perfect sense, Paula. Look around, bloody concrete everywhere.

PAULA: Why don't you start now?

GARY: 'Cause I need this time.

Her phone rings.

Why you gettin' on my case about this?

PAULA: Shit. It's *him*.

GARY: Him him?

PAULA: Yep.

She silences the ring.

GARY: So?

PAULA: So what?

GARY: So what do you wanta do?

PAULA: About what?

GARY: Him.

PAULA: Nothing.

GARY: Maybe we could—

PAULA: What?

GARY: I don't know… you could…?

PAULA: NO!

GARY: Come on, Paula, even up the score.

PAULA: Fuck no, Gary.

GARY: Why not?

PAULA: He's a prick, that's why.

GARY: Just this once then we're done.

PAULA: It's not just us around here next week.

GARY: Yeah yeah, but that's next week.

PAULA: I mean it. I don't want you hangin' round the place all day.

GARY: What do you mean?

Her phone rings again.

Paula.

PAULA: Shit.

GARY: Have they said something to you already?

PAULA: No.

GARY: They hate it that I make you happy.

PAULA: Shit.

GARY: It's true.

PAULA: [*showing him the phone*] Him again. Jesus.

She silences the ring again.

Anyway, I don't want to talk about it now. I gotta go to work.

GARY: They manipulate you, Paula.

PAULA: They don't manipulate me.

GARY: They fucking well do and you give 'em what they want. Then they come back in here and walk all over you.

PAULA: It's not just about them.

GARY: Yes it fuckin well is!

PAULA: Don't lose it.

GARY: I'm not losin' it.

PAULA: You're about to lose it.

GARY: I'm not losin' it.

The dog starts barking.

I swear, that dog.

PAULA: Dogs bark.

GARY: It barks at me when I get home. Can't even recognise its owner. [*To the dog*] The hand that bloody feeds ya. I swear I'll kill that / mongrel if it...

PAULA: We got together over that dog.

GARY: ... well, if it doesn't bloody shut up it might be the end of us.

PAULA: Don't, Gary.
    Look, babe: I love you. You know that. I just want you out from under my feet. That's all.

GARY: Did they say that?

PAULA: It's never been the best with them... / you know that.

GARY: Yeah, but did they say that?

    The phone rings.

    They did... I swear—Shut up, Joey!

PAULA: Right, that's it.

    She answers it.

    It's over, Ray!
    Nup. Fuck off, Ray.
    Yeah, I'm upset.
    You're here!?
    [*Mouthing to* GARY *with hand over the phone*] (He's fucking here.)

GARY: Oh, Jesus.

PAULA: No! (Out the front.)

    She waves at GARY *to have a look.*

GARY: (What the fuck?!)

PAULA: Are you on your own?

GARY: (He is. / He is.)

PAULA: We told you last time—No no no. Which part of that—what? (GARY: Tell him to fuck off.

PAULA: I am.

GARY: Tell him again.)

    We can hear RAY *outside the door.*

RAY: [*off*] ... she's had a bad bout of bronchitis but she's much better now... / she's on her way.

GARY: He's fuckin' ... / FUCK OFF, RAY!

PAULA: No, Ray. / Fuck off.

RAY: [*off*] She'll be here / in a few minutes.

PAULA: Now's not the right / time.

RAY: [*off*] I was in the area. / It's all come together.

(GARY: Did you ask him to come?

PAULA: No. Fuck no.)

RAY: [*off*] If you just let me in we can have a drink and wait. Maybe get started and she can join in when she gets here. How much time have we got?

> RAY *knocks on the door.*

GARY: No time, mate. Daisy's gotta go to work. / We're busy.

RAY: [*off*] I sent you a text / on my way.

PAULA: We didn't get it.

GARY: Wait out there, Ray, and when the girl comes you can knock again. (She's not comin'. He's a fuckin' liar.)

> *He knocks again.*

> *The dog barks louder.*

RAY: [*off*] Come on.

PAULA: This is the second time / you've come without her.

RAY: [*off*] I'm not fucking you round, mate.

PAULA: How do we know that, hunh Ray?

GARY: (Hang up. Jesus.)

RAY: [*off*] It's your turn this time, Gary. Trust me. / I'll be on my best behaviour.

GARY: (Can you believe this?) Nope, mate. It's not going to happen!

PAULA: I'm hanging up now, Ray. Okay.

> *She hangs up.*

I've hung up.

> RAY *knocks.*

RAY: [*off*] Let me in and I can explain.

GARY: I'm being polite now, Ray, and asking you to leave us alone. (Go and shut that fucking dog up, will you?

> PAULA *goes out.*

The neighbours will be round here.)

PAULA: [*off*] Hey, Joey. Come here, Joey. It's okay, matey. Come here.

That's it.

The dog stops.

PAULA *enters again.*

What's he doing?

Silence.

GARY: I don't know, maybe he's going back to the car.
PAULA: Maybe he's going.

The phone rings again.

The dog starts barking.

GARY: Don't answer that. Hang that thing up. Nah… Jesus. I mean it this time.

GARY *opens the door.*

PAULA: Gary, don't go out there… / Ohhhh! Jesus, Gary!

GARY *exits.*

GARY: I'm telling him to fuck off— [*Off*] Just fuck off now, Ray. I mean it. Fuck off.

The phone rings again.

The dog keeps barking.

PAULA *goes out to attend to the dog again.*

PAULA: JOEY. COME HERE. COME HERE, JOEY. YOU LITTLE SHIT.

The dog stops barking.

Good boy.

Blackout.

2. ONE WEEK BEFORE

MICHAEL *is sitting in the dark.* AMY *enters.*

AMY: [*startled*] Jesus.
MICHAEL: Hi.
AMY: What are you doing?
MICHAEL: Grapefruit?

AMY: Turn on a light.
MICHAEL: I'm fine.
AMY: Okay. Weirdo.

>   *He takes a mouthful.*

Good?
MICHAEL: Uh-huh. Grapefruit and sugar. The perfect balance of sweet and sour.
AMY: Are you waiting for someone?
MICHAEL: Yes.
AMY: Who?
MICHAEL: You.
AMY: So I'm here.
What is it?
MICHAEL: I was going through the trash yesterday—
AMY: The trash… what trash?
MICHAEL: On the computer.
AMY: What computer?
MICHAEL: The computer in my office and I found something—
AMY: What were you doing trawling through the trash?
MICHAEL: It's my computer.
AMY: What were you looking for?
MICHAEL: I was looking for something of mine.

>   *Slight pause.*

AMY: What did you find?
MICHAEL: A photo.
AMY: What photo?
MICHAEL: Of you.
AMY: What photo of me?
MICHAEL: Come on, I don't need to tell you 'what photo'—
AMY: There's probably hundreds of photos of me on there.
MICHAEL: We both know.
AMY: Do we?
MICHAEL: Don't make me describe it.
AMY: Well, go on then, why don't you?
MICHAEL: I'm not going to.
AMY: After all, you went looking.

MICHAEL: I didn't go… not for that photo I didn't.
   So?
AMY: What?
   I don't know what you're talking about.
MICHAEL: Amy. I'm / trying to—
AMY: DESCRIBE IT.
MICHAEL: You want me to describe it?
AMY: Yes.
MICHAEL: Well, I'm not going to.

   Slight pause.

AMY: Go on, you sick fuck.
MICHAEL: What is it with you these days… don't you talk to me / like
   that.
AMY: Describe it.

   Pause.

MICHAEL: I just want to / talk to—
AMY: Not until you tell me what you saw.
MICHAEL: Oh, Jesu— Okay. What I saw.
AMY: Yes.
MICHAEL: Fuck you, Amy.
AMY: That's the spirit.
MICHAEL: You're sitting on my work chair.
AMY: In the office?
MICHAEL: In the office. Yes. Legs…
AMY: What?
MICHAEL: Legs…
AMY: Akimbo.
MICHAEL: Your feet up on my desk.
AMY: Touching myself. Was I touching myself? On your leather chair?
   In your office?
MICHAEL: Yes.
AMY: You have a photo of that?
MICHAEL: Yes.

   Pause.

AMY: Okay. Well. We're talking about the same photo then.

Pause.

Have you told Mum?

MICHAEL: No. No I haven't.

Did you send it?

AMY: What?

MICHAEL: That photo?

AMY: Yes.

MICHAEL: Who to?

AMY: A boy.

MICHAEL: Jesus, Amy, you can see your face.

AMY: The best bit.

MICHAEL: It might be the best bit but it's hardly the focus.

AMY: I suppose not.

MICHAEL: Who is he?

AMY: Someone I know.

MICHAEL: How well do you know him?

AMY: Well enough.

MICHAEL: Really?

How do you know him?

AMY: From around?

MICHAEL: School.

AMY: No, he's left school.

MICHAEL: He's older... how much older?

AMY: A few years.

MICHAEL: How many years?

AMY: Ten.

MICHAEL: Ten years. And how do you know what he's doing with these photos?

AMY: He tells me what he does.

MICHAEL: And what's that?

AMY: Use your imagination.

MICHAEL: My imagination is not something I'm trying to exercise at the moment.

AMY: Why not?

MICHAEL: Because I don't want to think where those photos have ended up.

AMY: Where would they end up?

MICHAEL: You know where.

AMY: He sends me photos too.

MICHAEL: I'm sure he does.

AMY: Do you want to see them?

MICHAEL: No!

AMY: I was just asking… seeing as you're so curious.

    Pause.

MICHAEL: Don't you see why I might be a bit concerned?

    Pause.

  Do you?

  So what's going on with this guy?

AMY: I don't know… I like him.

MICHAEL: Have you met him?

AMY: No.

MICHAEL: You haven't met him but you've sent him—

AMY: Yes.

MICHAEL: How do you know you like him?

AMY: What he says.

MICHAEL: You mean what he says online?

AMY: Yes.

MICHAEL: Are you going to meet him?

AMY: I might.

MICHAEL: Depending on what?

  What?

AMY: That's private.

MICHAEL: Oh, that bit's private.

AMY: Yes.

MICHAEL: Right. Well, I want to say—and I don't say this often—I never say this—you know that—but I—

AMY: Disapprove.

MICHAEL: Yes—

AMY: I'm sorry I used your computer, Dad, mine's got a shitty camera.

    Slight pause.

MICHAEL: It's got nothing to do with whose computer—

AMY: If I had one with a better camera we wouldn't be having this conversation.

MICHAEL: I'm glad we're having this conversation.

AMY: You don't look that glad.

MICHAEL: I'm in shock.

AMY: Don't be. Not on my account anyway.

MICHAEL: I don't think you should meet him.

AMY: You can't decide that / for me.

MICHAEL: I'll ask you again. How well do you know him?

AMY: As well as anyone.

MICHAEL: As well as me? As well as your mother?

AMY: I don't know, you tell me.

MICHAEL: I am not the one under suspicion—

AMY: Oh, no? Why don't we? Why don't we put your life under the microscope for a second? Why don't we trawl through your trash and see what we uncover? Why don't we do that?

MICHAEL: I invite you.

AMY: Do you? Do you really?

    Silence.

Well, I'd prefer not to be interrogated like this.

MICHAEL: I'm not prying, I'm trying to take care of you.

AMY: It's hard to tell the difference—

MICHAEL: Let me remind you: until you leave / this house—

AMY: Which might be sooner rather than later.

MICHAEL: Be that as it may. While you're under my roof—

AMY: You're responsible for my wellbeing.

MICHAEL: Yes.

AMY: I can take care of myself.

MICHAEL: Well, going on what I've seen I'm not so sure about that.

AMY: What are you suggesting actually?

MICHAEL: I'm not suggesting anything—

AMY: Yes you are.

MICHAEL: No I'm / not.

AMY: That I'm a slut. That I'm whoring myself around. Your little princess's not what she seems. Is that what you're worried about? Because you don't know anything about me.

MICHAEL: I am not suggesting or saying that / at all.

AMY: And you're worried what might happen to stupid girls who meet strange older men.

MICHAEL: What does this guy do?

AMY: He's a doctor.

MICHAEL: Oh, come on.

AMY: You don't believe me.

MICHAEL: I don't believe him.

AMY: I do.

MICHAEL: Studying to be a gynaecologist, I suppose.

AMY: That's in poor taste.

MICHAEL: I don't think you're the one in any position to be telling me about poor taste.

AMY: In a few months I'll be doing medicine.

MICHAEL: It's got nothing to do with that—

AMY: Yes it does.

MICHAEL: I fail to see—

AMY: Because you don't listen.

MICHAEL: I'm your father.

AMY: Fathers can listen too.

MICHAEL: Sometimes you'd do well to listen to me—for once.

AMY: Listen to me—

MICHAEL: You have not the first clue about the world.

AMY: Don't patronise me.

MICHAEL: So if you think I'm going to stand by—

AMY: Dad, listen!

MICHAEL: I'll listen when—

AMY: JUST FUCKING SHUT UP AND LISTEN, 'CAUSE I'M GOING TO STUDY MEDICINE—

MICHAEL: You're not there yet—

AMY: I'm gonna get in—then I'm going to start making decisions—decisions about people's lives—decisions you can't help me with—SO LISTEN.

Just fucking listen.

Pause.

MICHAEL: This isn't trivial, because I'm… believe me… Okay, I'm listening.

AMY: Spare me, will you? You're worse than 'A Current Affair'. I know all the arguments. I can hear them before they even come out of your mouth: Be careful, Amy. You don't know what he really wants from you?

He might lure me. Rape me, brutalise me, dump me in a ditch. You play the scenario out in your head. You think I'm safe in my room. A call comes. You don't recognise the number. Are you Michael Devine? We've found your daughter. What? Mum's panicking, she wants to know. Who is it? You know what the news is. Suddenly you don't recognise yourself. There's you listening and responding; and there's you somewhere else. Gone. Then, suddenly, there's a knock on the door.

3. FOUR DAYS AFTER

ANNE *in a very bright single light, smoking.*

ANNE: I'm sorry. I'll just finish this.

> *She takes one more drag, goes to put it out, then takes one last drag and butts it out.*

This light is very bright. Does it need to be…?

VOICE: Can we pull it down a fraction please?

How's that?

ANNE: Much better. Thank you.

VOICE: You just about ready, Mrs Devine?

ANNE: I can't guarantee I'm going to make it through… you know… without…

VOICE: It's okay.

ANNE: I'll try but…

VOICE: If you cry, just stop. We'll pick up where you left off and cut around later.

ANNE: I've got it written down… God, am I looking…? I feel…

VOICE: The camera loves you. You look great.

Right. Are you ready, Mrs Devine?

ANNE: As ready as I'll ever be.

VOICE: Remember, stop if you need to. There's no drama.

ANNE: No drama. Okay.

I'm ready.

VOICE: I'll count you in. Okay?

ANNE: Okay.
VOICE: Three. Two. One.
    You're on.

> *Silence.*

> *She breaks down.*

ANNE: Sorry.
VOICE: It's okay.
ANNE: I'll try and pick it up…
    Sorry.

> *Blackout.*

4. THREE MINUTES AFTER

PAULA. *The sound of a running tap and scrubbing.* GARY *enters, with a hammer.*

Silence.

PAULA: Wash your hands.
GARY: I just did.
PAULA: I didn't see you.
GARY: You heard me. I washed them.
PAULA: Really?
GARY: Look. Smell.

> *She smells his hands.*

> *Silence.*

    Joey's stopped.
PAULA: He stopped straight away.

> *Silence.*

    What are you going to do with that?
GARY: What?
PAULA: That?
GARY: I don't know. Put it…
    I don't know.
PAULA: Don't put it anywhere.
GARY: We have to put it somewhere.

PAULA: Not in here.
GARY: I'll put it back in the shed.
PAULA: Is it clean?
GARY: I cleaned it.

　　　GARY *laughs.*

PAULA: Don't laugh, Gary.
GARY: Cleaned the hammer…

　　　He shakes his head.

　　　[*Trying not to laugh*] I'm going to / put this—
PAULA: Don't—
GARY: I / won't.
PAULA: Please don't fucking laugh.
GARY: I won't laugh. I don't know what else I'm supposed to do.
　　But I… won't laugh.
　　Okay.
　　No laughing.

　　　Silence.

PAULA: Are you going to put it back?
GARY: Are you going to work?
PAULA: I'm meeting Jen at… What did I say? 6.30? Shit. I should go.
GARY: You should.
　　We shouldn't change anything.
　　Don't you think?

　　　Silence.

PAULA: Did you check again?
GARY: When?
PAULA: Before you came in before.
GARY: No.
PAULA: Why not?
GARY: 'Cause I checked I don't know how many times.
PAULA: How many?
GARY: You saw me.
PAULA: I can't remember.
GARY: Fuck. It doesn't matter… how many times is not the point.
PAULA: Check again.

GARY: No.

PAULA: Go in there.

GARY: Jesus, I'm not going in there again.

PAULA: How do we know?

GARY: Because I checked.

I mean...

Jesus.

He almost vomits.

Shit.

He vomits and runs offstage.

5. THE MORNING OF

JULIA WHITE. *A toilet flushes.* DAVID WHITE *enters doing up his belt.*

DAVID: Still here, Julia.

JULIA: Why wouldn't I be?

DAVID: I don't know. Where's he gone... / our man?

JULIA: Fuck: Look at yourself, David—

DAVID: What?

JULIA: What are you wearing?

DAVID: What was I supposed to wear?

JULIA: Anything that keeps your arse out of view.

DAVID: You can't see my—well... If I do this... [*bending over*] you definitely can. Or if I reach up like this [*reaching up*]. But I promise I won't do that. No... [*reaching up*] or... [*bending over*]. Okay.

JULIA: What's happened to you?

DAVID: Unemployment's done wonders, don't you think?

JULIA: Did you think this morning, 'Maybe I should put on a decent shirt, or a pair of pants'? Because it's not like you don't have them.

DAVID: No.

JULIA: No, you don't have them; or no, you didn't think?

DAVID: No, I've got them; yes, I thought about it.

JULIA: You did think about it.

DAVID: Yes.

JULIA: And that's what you decided.

DAVID: I was going to deodorise but apathy got in the way.

JULIA: Apathy for what?

DAVID: A severe disinclination for the rituals of personal grooming.

JULIA: So this is what you decided on—

DAVID: I knew you'd make an effort.

> MICHAEL *enters.*

Ahhh. There he is.

MICHAEL: Feel free to take a look around… I'll be one minute. I've just got to…

> *He points to his phone.*

DAVID: No hurry. I've got all day.

> MICHAEL *gives the thumbs up and leaves.*

JULIA: Did you call James this morning?

DAVID: No.

JULIA: He asked you to call him.

DAVID: He did.

JULIA: Was that a choice?

DAVID: I can't stand his… 'concerned tone'.

JULIA: Maybe he is concerned.

DAVID: He's smug, not concerned. I can decipher that much.

JULIA: You haven't got a job—

DAVID: I know that.

JULIA: And whose fault is that?

DAVID: You think it's mine?

JULIA: At the time—

DAVID: At the time there was a 'downturn'.

JULIA: There certainly has been.

DAVID: I like to think of it as 'enlightenment'.

JULIA: You'd say that even after six months?

DAVID: Lucky I was earning a lot of money at the time.

JULIA: It's not luck or enlightenment.

DAVID: What do you want?

JULIA: I want you to show some interest… / some fight.

DAVID: For what?

JULIA: For your life. Our life.

DAVID: I'm here, aren't I?

JULIA: In some ways.

DAVID: Fuck you, you know that—

JULIA: Being here isn't enough. It's how you present. It's your entire being that I'm reading, David.

DAVID: My 'entire being'.

JULIA: That's right.

DAVID: My clothes being a representation of my 'entire being'.

JULIA: You could say that.

DAVID: Would you say that?

Because I don't think. I don't feel. I only dress… dress up a corpse.

MICHAEL *enters.*

MICHAEL: One more minute, I promise.

MICHAEL *gives the thumbs up.* DAVID *gives him the thumbs up back.*

DAVID: [*to* MICHAEL] You're right, mate.

MICHAEL *exits, indicating they should look around.*

JULIA: What do you think you look like?

DAVID: A fat fucking slob. But inside I'm a deeply caring man. Deeply. I can assure you.

JULIA: Can you?

DAVID: Yes. I can. I can.

Silence.

And what do you look like?

JULIA: What do you mean, what do I look like?

DAVID: What do you think you look like?

JULIA: I look like I always look.

DAVID: How's that?

JULIA: Why don't you tell me what you think?

DAVID: No, because we're playing a game of self-appraisal.

JULIA: I see.

DAVID: Don't tell me what you think I think. Tell me honestly. What do you look like?

JULIA: Like someone who's meant to be here.

DAVID: Dressed for entitlement. I see.

A severe fucking bitch.

JULIA: What?

DAVID: That's what you look like.

JULIA: I didn't ask you.

DAVID: No, but you didn't have to.

>	*Pause.*

>	MICHAEL *enters.*

MICHAEL: Right. David. Julia. I'm sorry to keep you waiting.

6. FOUR DAYS AFTER

ANNE. AMY *enters.*

AMY: What are you talking about, Mum, you came across really well.

ANNE: Did I?

AMY: Absolutely.

ANNE: They said the camera loves me.

AMY: Well, I'm not sure about that.
    You were graceful under pressure.

ANNE: I can always rely on you to be honest. It's his birthday today. I got him a watch.

AMY: Did they confirm he was in Melbourne?

ANNE: They spoke to one of his clients there.
    I'm giving them full access to the office and computer here.

AMY: Why?

ANNE: What else can I do?

AMY: Do you really want them to see everything?

ANNE: I've got nothing to hide.

>	*Slight pause.*

    Did he say anything to you?

AMY: What?

ANNE: I don't know. That he was unhappy? That he wanted to leave?

AMY: No, Mum.

ANNE: Because I just put myself out there.

AMY: I know… I've told you / everything.

ANNE: Don't lie to me, Amy.

AMY: I'm not lying to you.

ANNE: I mean it.

AMY: Mum—

ANNE: Because this is not funny.

AMY: I'm not / laughing.

ANNE: I'm not going to be the one laughed at.

AMY: No-one's laughing at you.

ANNE: You'd better not be.

AMY: Why would / I—

ANNE: I won't be humiliated—you hear me. I won't be the last person to find out.

AMY: Mum.

ANNE: I won't be taken / for a ride.

AMY: Jesus, no-one's—

ANNE: I will not.

AMY: I'm not lying to you. Why would you think that? Why would you even think that?

ANNE: Because you were close to him. You were always closer to him. You didn't notice anything… hear him talking to anyone?

AMY: No. We've been through all this—

ANNE: I've literally put my hand in every pocket, on every chit of paper, every stray phone number. Been through the rubbish under his desk. Receipts. Files on his computer. The lot.

I just don't understand. I don't understand where he's gone.

AMY: Neither do I.

ANNE: Did I give him any reason… what's that look?

AMY: Nothing. / There's no—

ANNE: What is it?

AMY: I don't know what to say / that's all—

ANNE: You don't know what to say because you don't know how to say it?

AMY: No.

ANNE: Did you speak about me?

AMY: We didn't actually.

ANNE: Come on, Amy, I'm not stupid.

AMY: I know you're not—

ANNE: Was he seeing someone else?

AMY: I don't know, Mum. That's not something I know… or really want to… I don't know… I'm on his computer sometimes.

ANNE: What?

AMY: I mean I use it for some things.

There was some porn… once… he'd forgotten to close the tab.

ANNE: That's it?

Slight pause.

I saw that.

AMY: Do you know Lauren Cleary?

ANNE: She was his last girlfriend before we met.

AMY: There was an email from her.

ANNE: They keep in touch.

AMY: That's all. That's all I know.

7. *THE MORNING OF*

Return to the display home—JULIA, DAVID *and* MICHAEL.

MICHAEL: That was my wife. My flight's been delayed. I just had to call her. If I don't let her know she worries, you know—those 'unaccounted for' hours.

DAVID: She lives in Sydney?

MICHAEL: She does.

DAVID: [*for* JULIA*'s benefit*] Have you got children, Michael?

MICHAEL: Yes I do.

DAVID: How many?

MICHAEL: One.

DAVID: Only one.

MICHAEL: Unfortunately.

DAVID: Still. One. One's better than none, isn't it, Julia? You didn't want any more?

MICHAEL: My wife had a… difficult pregnancy. We didn't want to risk it again.

DAVID: Sorry to hear that.

MICHAEL: We've moved on.

DAVID: Have you?

MICHAEL: I think so. Yes.

DAVID: Julia's a doctor.

MICHAEL: Are you?

JULIA: I am.
DAVID: Intensive care.
MICHAEL: My wife owes her life to the doctors.
   Anyway, enough about me. Did you have a quick look…?
DAVID: No. We were… chatting.
MICHAEL: Right then. Can I?
JULIA: You can.
DAVID: We're all yours.
MICHAEL: I'll be gentle.

> *They laugh.*

> DAVID *and* MICHAEL *leave.*

> JULIA *stays back.*

8. ONE MONTH AFTER

ANNE *and her* PSYCHIATRIST, DR ANDREWS.

PSYCHIATRIST: Anne.
ANNE: Dr Andrews. Hi. Fuck.
PSYCHIATRIST: It's okay.
ANNE: I'm sorry I'm late.
PSYCHIATRIST: It doesn't matter.
ANNE: I had it in my diary…
PSYCHIATRIST: Really. Do you want to sit down, Mrs Devine?
ANNE: Anne.

> *She stays standing.*

   I really got stuck into your secretary before.
PSYCHIATRIST: She's used to it.
ANNE: Is she?
PSYCHIATRIST: We don't encourage it. But it happens.
ANNE: I'll apologise to her.
PSYCHIATRIST: I'm sure she'd appreciate it.
ANNE: She didn't lose her cool once.
PSYCHIATRIST: She never does.
ANNE: It's really annoying actually.
PSYCHIATRIST: Really?

ANNE: Really fucking annoying.

   I'm swearing a lot lately.

PSYCHIATRIST: That's hardly surprising considering.

ANNE: No, I guess not.

PSYCHIATRIST: Would you like to sit down?

ANNE: I suppose you know everything. Read the lot.

PSYCHIATRIST: I don't know you at all—

ANNE: Let's not pretend.

PSYCHIATRIST: I mean it.

ANNE: I've got used to a certain notoriety these days.

PSYCHIATRIST: I know a few… what?… facts. But I don't know you,
   Anne. And I wouldn't presume. I was thinking we could run over
   time—

ANNE: No, it's okay.

PSYCHIATRIST: I've got lunch after this and I don't mind taking / a few
   minutes.

ANNE: I don't want to put you out.

PSYCHIATRIST: You're not putting me out. It's a quiet day. I've had a few
   no-shows.

ANNE: That's nice.

   Do you always wear that to work?

PSYCHIATRIST: I'm sorry.

ANNE: Do you always dress… you know?

PSYCHIATRIST: Down?

ANNE: Yes.

PSYCHIATRIST: What reason do I have to 'dress up'?

ANNE: I don't know, I suppose. Perception.

       Pause.

   I suppose not.

PSYCHIATRIST: Did you dress up to be here?

ANNE: You mean… no. This is what I wear. I freshened up. You know.

PSYCHIATRIST: Well, I'm glad you made it today.

ANNE: Are you?

PSYCHIATRIST: I am.

ANNE: I've never… seen anyone before.

       Pause.

Never had the need. My life's been... fortunate. I suppose you could say.

PSYCHIATRIST: It's really something—believe me—to hear that.

ANNE: You would deal more with the un-fortunate.

PSYCHIATRIST: You could say that.

ANNE: Come ye all and understand your mis-fortunes.

Do you believe in fortune... I mean that some things are genuinely out of your control?

PSYCHIATRIST: It depends very much on the circumstances.

ANNE: In the main, though, do you endeavour to make your patients understand their role in their misfortunes? How they might have brought it upon themselves.

PSYCHIATRIST: I don't trade in guilt, if that's what you mean.

ANNE: But this is a type of confession.

PSYCHIATRIST: Revelation.

ANNE: For who? Who's revealed?

PSYCHIATRIST: Well. You. I hope.

9. FIVE MINUTES AFTER

PAULA. GARY *enters.*

GARY: Did I...?

Paula?

PAULA: No.

GARY: What else could've I done?

PAULA: Nothing.

GARY: Are you sure?

PAULA: Yes.

GARY: You saw it?

PAULA: I did. Everything.

GARY: Everything.

10. ONE MONTH AFTER

ANNE *and her* PSYCHIATRIST.

Silence.

ANNE: I don't know what to say.

PSYCHIATRIST: You don't have to say anything.

ANNE: We have to talk about something.

PSYCHIATRIST: No we don't.

ANNE: You mean…

PSYCHIATRIST: I mean I always make it very clear—to everyone—when they come through that door—silence is just as valid as anything you say.

Time. You see. We have time.

ANNE: Yes. I'm paying for it.

PSYCHIATRIST: You are.

ANNE: Can I… [*indicating she'd like to lie down*]?

The PSYCHIATRIST *gestures approval.*

ANNE *lies down.*

Oh God, that's good. You know how long it's been since I laid down in the middle of the day?

It's amazing what you can get when you pay for it. Amazing.

PSYCHIATRIST: What do you mean?

ANNE: Is this what it's going to be like?

PSYCHIATRIST: What?

ANNE: You asking me, what I mean?

PSYCHIATRIST: Yes.

ANNE: Probing.

PSYCHIATRIST: Facilitating.

ANNE: Huh. Yes—probe. Not that savoury. If you were probing you'd have—what?—an instrument.

PSYCHIATRIST: I don't have anything.

ANNE: That I can see, anyway.

PSYCHIATRIST: Nothing. I swear.

They laugh.

ANNE: This room… there's something about it. You know… something familiar. I mean… you can walk into someone else's living room nowadays, a psychiatrist's office, a house completely on the other side of town and feel like you've walked into your own. It reminds me of my own living room.

PSYCHIATRIST: Sounds like you've thought about it.

ANNE: You could be completely distracted—checking a message on your phone—and walk right into a stranger's house—until the dog bites you, of course—the only one who knows you're intruding. Otherwise we could drift, completely unknown, right through each other's rooms... seeing faces we think we recognise... the faces of the people we love... who care for us... but really, what we should be asking is, if it's a mask, a mask over a pernicious, rotting life.

PSYCHIATRIST: Is that what you feel you're doing now?

11. SIX MINUTES AFTER

GARY *and* PAULA.

GARY: Can you smell...?

PAULA: What?

No.

GARY: Really?

PAULA: Nothing.

GARY: I thought I could... How long do you think?

PAULA: I don't know, Gary. How would I fuckin' know?

GARY: I'm just.

PAULA: I've got to go.

GARY: I know.

Go.

PAULA: Will you be okay?

GARY: Yeah, I'll be fine.

PAULA: You still feeling sick?

GARY: Yep.

PAULA: Call me if...

GARY: I will.

He was never supposed to...

PAULA: I know.

GARY: Did you invite him?

PAULA: Of course I didn't.

GARY: You sure?

PAULA: Fuck off, Gary.

GARY: Did he send you a text?

PAULA: What?

GARY: To say he was comin'?

PAULA: I haven't checked.

GARY: Check, Paula. Fuckin' check.

PAULA: Okay.

GARY: Who does he think we are? He's the fuckin' whatever he said.

PAULA: He sent this.

GARY: *You two randy sex rats. I'm on my way over. She'll meet me at yours. See you in 15. Ray. xx.*

That's it.

PAULA: Exactly.

GARY: I'm sorry. I'm so sorry. I'm the one that suggested all this.

PAULA: Don't.

GARY: Why wouldn't he leave?

PAULA: I don't know.

GARY: I asked him how many times?

PAULA: We both did.

GARY: You heard me.

PAULA: I did.

GARY: How many?

PAULA: Jesus, Gary.

GARY: What?

PAULA: The kids are coming next week.

My fucking kids.

Pause.

GARY: I know. I know. Come here.

PAULA: I mean it.

GARY: It's my fuckin' fault I know.

PAULA: Fuck, Gary. Pull yourself together. Alright. Just stop it.

Pause.

We can't rewind. How does it look? Think about that. For once in your life, think. We need to know exactly how this looks for us?

12. ONE MONTH AFTER

ANNE *and her* PSYCHIATRIST.

ANNE: I can't sleep replaying every little thing. That morning—the last morning—

PSYCHIATRIST: Before your husband?

ANNE: Yes. He was on the first flight to Melbourne. We were always restless on those mornings, waiting for the alarm to go off. Just lying there... awake. It was hot. He reached out and touched me... on the stomach. Very softly. We've been married a long time... and he's still touching me. It felt good. We made love... then he's running late. A bit of a panic to get him out the door. He'd misplaced some papers.

PSYCHIATRIST: What papers?

ANNE: That's exactly it: what papers? You keep asking yourself—every minute of the day—What did I miss? How could I've been so stupid? I packed his bag upstairs, while he looked for the papers. He wasn't looking for any papers... or maybe he was. I don't know. You see? I don't know anymore. I scrutinise every single detail... every single word... every touch. It felt like my husband. But how can you actually know? What's going on in his head? Maybe that morning he really was touching me... he really was making love to me. But you can never know. There's no hard evidence. And that's what makes me sick. That... that gap. That unknowable... untraceable gap.

Twenty years of marriage and the whole thing is like a dream... one I'm trying to wake up in... to make real... but I can't.

PSYCHIATRIST: You mean, you can't wake up and see it for what it really is?

ANNE: No, because there was my husband and then there was somebody else.

13. SEVEN MINUTES AFTER

GARY *and* PAULA.

PAULA: [*putting down her bag*] Right. Fuck this, Gary. We have to decide. Some people might say we're a bit sick for what we do. But that's our choice. We were clear with him from the beginning. Then we both saw what happened.

GARY: I lost it. I lost my stupid fucking temper.

PAULA: But this is our house. We're entitled to defend it, aren't we?

GARY: We never invited him.

PAULA: Never.

GARY: He comes barging in here.

A phone rings offstage.

Is that his?

They let it ring out.

So what do we do about that?

Her phone rings.

PAULA: Shit. It's Jenny. I can't go to fucking work.

GARY: Answer it.

PAULA: You answer it. Tell her I'm sick.

GARY: You have to speak to her.

PAULA: Okay. Jenny. Hi.

You there already?

Yeah, I'm on my way. I got caught up—

Nah, I'm coming. On my way now.

Twenty minutes… that okay? I'm sorry, Jenny.

Yeah… tell you all about when I get there.

Yep. 'Bye.

She hangs up.

GARY: I can't think straight.

PAULA: If we're gonna call the cops, we have to do it now, we can't wait any longer. It looks bad if we wait. And if we don't ring them then…

Slight pause.

GARY: Okay, tell me quickly… so we both know… so we're straight… tell me everything from the beginning… everything you remember.

14. ONE WEEK BEFORE

AMY *and* MICHAEL.

MICHAEL: I know what it sounds like.

AMY: Then why say it?

MICHAEL: Because when you're a father—

AMY: I'm not going to be a father.

MICHAEL: You know what I mean—

AMY: No I don't.

MICHAEL: What's got into you, Amy—apart from the photographs—I'm not speaking about them now—over the past year—you're curt—you're short with me—you're… you're—

AMY: A bitch.

MICHAEL: Yes.

AMY: I am.

MICHAEL: You are.

AMY: I'm just sick of everyone's presumptions.

MICHAEL: What about?

AMY: About my life.

MICHAEL: What about it?

AMY: Every part of it.

MICHAEL: For example.

AMY: No-one really wants to get to know me.

MICHAEL: I do.

AMY: But you don't.

MICHAEL: I don't know what I should and shouldn't ask.

AMY: You're afraid to find out.

MICHAEL: Well, do you blame me going on what I've recently uncovered? I'll think twice before I go trawling through the trash.

AMY: Actually, maybe you shouldn't.

MICHAEL: Think twice?

AMY: Maybe people are afraid their ideas will shatter, their precious little ideas. But more ideas need to smash, I reckon. They need to be smashed down. Pulverised. 'Cause I fucking hate them. I mean it.

MICHAEL: I know you do.

AMY: The image you have of me in your head—your daughter—it's not worth anything.

MICHAEL: Is that really true?

AMY: You want me to do medicine, but you don't want me naked in your office, masturbating for another man, looking down the camera, looking straight back at you—you don't want to see that, do you!?

MICHAEL: It's not because I'm afraid of you.

AMY: What?

MICHAEL: I'm afraid for you.

AMY: WELL, DON'T BE. DON'T BE AFRAID FOR ME. THAT'S EXACTLY WHAT I'M FUCKING SAYING. WHAT ARE YOU AFRAID OF? REALLY? TELL ME.

Silence.

I don't know why... I want to keep him interested... I suppose.

MICHAEL: Who?

AMY: This guy.

MICHAEL: This guy you send—

AMY: Yes. And then I'm... AHHH! Suddenly... I'm slutting myself.

MICHAEL: No, Amy, you're not.

AMY: Go on.

MICHAEL: You are not slutting / yourself.

AMY: You can say it.

MICHAEL: There's nothing to say.

AMY: I know you think it.

MICHAEL: No.

AMY: Dad.

MICHAEL: It's alright.

AMY: I'm lost. Like, really lost. And I can't find my way back.

MICHAEL: What do you mean?

AMY: There's me, the person you know, then there's this other person... this thing... I don't even know what it is... that makes me...

MICHAEL: You mean the photo?

AMY: Yes. But it's not just that.

I do know this guy.

MICHAEL: The guy who you chat to.

AMY: Yes. We meet all the time.

MICHAEL: I thought you said you hadn't met.

AMY: I just wanted to annoy you.

MICHAEL: Okay.

AMY: I want to have sex with him.

MICHAEL: Well... You don't have to ask my permission.

AMY: I'm not asking you. I'm scared.

MICHAEL: Of what?

AMY: Of falling in love with him.

MICHAEL: Have you been in love before?

AMY: I have.

MICHAEL: I didn't know. Did you tell your mum?

AMY: No.

MICHAEL: Right.

Who was he, Amy? Do I know him?

AMY: It doesn't matter. We were around at his place one night… getting drunk. We had these film clips on and I was dancing around to one of them… I was crawling along the floor, chasing him… you know… like a dog… it was a game. I caught him and I bit him. I bit him harder than I thought… I don't really know what happened. But anyway then he grabbed me and said, 'Is that the way you want it?' I was laughing… you know… I thought it was a joke. But he bit me back. Hard. I mean… it really hurt… it drew blood. And he started laughing. But I wasn't. I told him to, 'Get off!' You know… 'Get off me!' And I suppose I was pretty angry, 'cause it shocked me and I was bleeding, but he was really angry too and I don't know why… but he pushed me as he was getting up off me and stood over me and spat. He spat right in my face. And I was like instantly 'Fuck you', you know, and I got up and I left… but I felt totally I don't know—

MICHAEL: Oh God, Amy… I'm…

AMY: Don't be. Don't be sorry for me. I'm alright.

MICHAEL: Really?

AMY: Really.

Please, Dad. Don't.

MICHAEL: Okay.

Silence.

AMY: So when are you going to buy a Prius?

MICHAEL: Right. From masturbation, to this… guy, to a Prius.

AMY: It's a logical progression.

So when?

15. THE MORNING OF

MICHAEL, JULIA *and* DAVID.

MICHAEL: So: we're back to where we started—the living room. And that's an 'in essence', bespoke home. As you can see from a quick look at the whole place, our architect, Haruki Fumhiko—you can read about him in the brochure there—he's gone for open spaces. There's a flexibility in the plan that enables every room, every aspect, every detail to become your unique expression. You bring to it exactly what you want. The world according to you. Look: none of this lifestyle rubbish. Life in 'your style'. If you see the difference.

People are calling this a new threshold of living. And look, you can call it what you like. Because there's you—the person, you know—that you're sold—that you feel you're meant to be—and then there's the other you: the person that knows—deep down—that there's nothing more precious than the relationships around you... and who'll do anything to protect that. A home should reflect that core value?

I mean... the GFC? What GFC? The so-called 'catastrophe'. Well, it might be a catastrophe but it's not critical... not if you're selling something real, something people really want, if you've got that something in your hands. That's why I'm still on the site, selling these things myself. Believe me, I could have someone else doing it. But I still get a buzz. You know. When I'm talking to people like you. Better than someone else selling something they don't believe in... for money. It degenerates then... falls into this... generic thing. And that's exactly what we don't want.

I might have mentioned it before but let me reiterate: the strata comes with comprehensive, Third-Eye security solutions—which includes 10 points of CCTV for every home, covering all major entrances and exits, bio-optic access recognition on doors and gates, linked to on-site security personnel... 24/7, as my daughter likes to say. A co-ordinated, armed response to any unidentified intrusion. To ensure you're with you and yours. Peace of mind. You know: hope for the best; prepare for the worst.

So what about you guys, if you don't mind me asking—Did I say double garage?

JULIA: You did.

MICHAEL: Goes without saying.—You're moving because of children?

DAVID: Maybe.

MICHAEL: Can I say something?

DAVID: I get the feeling you're going to anyway.

MICHAEL: Take it from me: have as many as you can. My daughter goes on about the population crisis. But it's not us. It's the Indians and the Chinese. What are we in Australia, 22, 23 million? Something like that. A drop in the ocean. I tell you, kids are their own greatest reward. Happiest day of my life when she was born. I can run through the features of a place. But what are they? They're features. I can't actually convince you of this and that. Ultimately it's your choice. How old are you—late 30s—I assume—so I don't have to say… you know: the clock is ticking. There's no right time. There's only a decision. They change your life. No question. I'd have three more if I could. Didn't work out that way. Lucky I have one.

So do you have any questions?

Pause.

DAVID: It's all fairly self-explanatory.

His phone rings. He looks at it.

It's James.

JULIA: Get it.

DAVID: Later.

JULIA: Now.

DAVID: [*rolling his eyes*] Here we go.

Excuse me.

James.

I know… I know. I was going to call you back.

What? I'm in a display home.

He exits.

Pause.

MICHAEL: Trouble?

JULIA: Sorry?

MICHAEL: Between the two of you. I sense… trouble.

JULIA: Could say that. He lost his job six months ago.

MICHAEL: I see.

It's none of my business, but…

JULIA: No no, it's okay.

MICHAEL: We've all been there.

JULIA: I suppose.

MICHAEL: Things feel like they're never going to change. The tedium.

JULIA: With each other.

MICHAEL: Mmm, you've got to make changes.

JULIA: Like?

MICHAEL: You're obviously looking to move.

JULIA: Well... we are...

MICHAEL: But it's more than that.

JULIA: It is.

MICHAEL: Can I ask you something?

JULIA: Ask away.

MICHAEL: Tell me if it's too much.

JULIA: Okay.

MICHAEL: Are you... thinking about other people?

JULIA: Huh...

> *She laughs.*

You mean?

MICHAEL: Yes.

Is that too forward?

JULIA: I don't...

> *Slight pause.*

No. It's not, actually. I think about people I don't know mainly. People I see on the street. Strangers.

MICHAEL: I'm asking because...

We don't have to be miserable all our lives. People are locked into an idea of themselves. Ideas that—how do you say it?—deprive them of their fantasies.

JULIA: I don't know if I'm following.

> DAVID *enters.*

MICHAEL: Do you ever feel like you're being watched?

Like... if you suddenly did something... something you'd barely admit to yourself... there'd be eyes on you... wondering who you really are? As if people suddenly won't recognise you. Accusing, judgmental eyes. That'll cast you out.

JULIA: Everyone fears that.

MICHAEL: And why is that?

JULIA: Shame.

MICHAEL: But who's to say there's anything actually wrong.

JULIA: With our fantasies?

MICHAEL: Who makes those decisions?
You know.

JULIA: I do. I'll think about it.

MICHAEL: Do that.
I think we're being watched.

JULIA: What did James say?

DAVID: There's nothing for me.

Pause.

JULIA: We probably just need a moment.

MICHAEL: I'll be out the front making a few calls. Give us a yell if there's anything you need.

DAVID: Thanks, Michael.

JULIA: Thanks.

MICHAEL: My pleasure. Oh, I have to head off in about… 20, if that's okay with you?

JULIA: Fine.

DAVID: No problems.

MICHAEL *leaves.*

Silence.

JULIA: You're a fucking prick.

DAVID *looks around the room.*

DAVID: I hate it.

JULIA: I don't recognise you anymore.
I really don't.

MICHAEL *enters.*

MICHAEL: Oh shit, I was going on before and forgot to say—the kitchen benches are Caesarstone—sorry—but, you know, we can put marble in, if that's what you want. The 'real' thing. Nothing like it.

JULIA: That's good to know.

MICHAEL *gives the thumbs up and exits again.*

16. TEN MINUTES AFTER

GARY *and* PAULA.

PAULA: I don't know, Gary, it's not that important.

GARY: No, every detail's important.

PAULA: Okay. Alright, you're right.

GARY: Okay. So you're on the phone.

PAULA: Yep and it's fucking stupid talking to him on the phone, when he's just standing outside the door, so you tell me to hang up, and you talk to him.

GARY: That's right. I told him again a deal's a deal—through the door.

PAULA: He wants to come in and wait. He's going on and on about it… this time the girl's on her way. Let me come in… we'll get started… something like that.

GARY: Fuck off, Ray! Knock again when she turns up.

PAULA: Yeah. That's what you said.

GARY: The fucking dog's barking. He's saying all sorts of shit, then—

PAULA: Then I'm out there with the dog and he goes back to the car, remember?

GARY: That's right.

PAULA: Shit, his car's still here.

GARY: Oh, shit. That's right.

He runs to the window.

PAULA: What sorta car does he have?

GARY: One of those hybrid fuckin' things—what are they called?—a Prius.

PAULA: What did he say he does?

GARY: Landscaping.

PAULA: Can you afford a Prius doing landscaping?

GARY: What was he wearing when he got here?

PAULA: Bit dressed-up for landscaping.

GARY: He could've come from the office.

PAULA: He bragged he was all hands-on.

GARY: Yeah. Who the fuck is this guy?

17. FIVE DAYS AFTER

ANNE *and the* DETECTIVE.

ANNE: You can call me Anne, detective. We're over the formalities now.

DETECTIVE: I know this is traumatic. But let me assure you, Anne, we're taking this extremely seriously. This is a fully co-ordinated response. We've referred the operation to the highest level... State Security. The Commissioner wants to be informed immediately of any developments.

ANNE: Because he's worried you haven't found anything, and he doesn't know what to say to the media.

DETECTIVE: That's one part of it. Now, I just need to go through it all once more, to make sure we've got it straight, so correct me if I'm wrong. He was in Melbourne on business. A message in his message bank from one of his clients there, a prospective buyer—she's considered the offer and would like to begin arrangements. He boarded flight QF317. CCTV footage of him carrying a plastic bag full of grapefruit in the Sydney airport, confirming he arrived on that flight, and that his plane landed on time. But you received a phone call from him saying it was delayed by an hour. That's right?

ANNE: Yes. That's right.

DETECTIVE: And his car was still parked at work?

> *Slight pause.*

We still don't know how he got to and from the airport.

ANNE: Taxis.

DETECTIVE: We assume.

ANNE: Well, he didn't walk.

DETECTIVE: There are two types of missing people: those who disappear willingly. And those who don't.

> *Pause.*

Someone called us before.

ANNE: Who?

DETECTIVE: A woman. Lauren Cleary. Do you know her?

ANNE: She's one of Michael's old friends.

DETECTIVE: Actually she claims to be more than a friend.

ANNE: They went out for three years before we were married.

DETECTIVE: She said they were having an affair.

ANNE: An affair what… you mean… now?

DETECTIVE: Yes.

ANNE: Until recently?

DETECTIVE: She saw you on television and thought she should come forward.

ANNE: What did she say?

DETECTIVE: I'm sorry to be the one telling / you this—

ANNE: Just say what you have to say, detective.

DETECTIVE: She said Michael was using another phone to keep in touch with her. At some point he lost that phone. Which was found and sold on with the same number. Miss Cleary called that old number, accidentally, and spoke to the new owner of the phone. He told her she wasn't the only person that'd been ringing that number looking for a man, a man who went by a variety of names, but all the callers wanted the same thing.

ANNE: What?

DETECTIVE: We also found this in his… well, your filing cabinet… in the office.

ANNE: What is it?

DETECTIVE: An advert in a magazine—*Vixsin*. It's a directory really. Buy it for $10 at a sex shop. Is that your husband?

ANNE: [*reading*] 'Looking for extremely friendly couple in their early 30s… who enjoy fully exploring the sexual ride of their lives. Not first timers… Only honest people need reply…'
Huh.

   Pause.

DETECTIVE: Is that Michael?

ANNE: Yes.

DETECTIVE: Do you know who the woman is?

ANNE: No. I don't.

DETECTIVE: Really?

ANNE: I've never seen her before.

DETECTIVE: Never?

ANNE: Never.

DETECTIVE: It's odd that he'd leave it lying around in a joint filing cabinet.

ANNE: I see. This is… right… when the investigation turns.

DETECTIVE: We just need to know what you and your / husband were up to.

ANNE: What we were up to? You think it's me. This woman. That we advertise for sex, Michael and I. You can't rule anything out, I suppose. I could have arranged this whole thing—I mean, let's face it, it's so bizarre it's unbelievable—that he just vanished off the face of the earth. Except I don't know who this woman is. Lauren Cleary. A prostitute. Some other vixen. I don't know. You see the problem is, I really am that wife—that devoted wife, with no proclivity for advertising myself naked in sex magazines. I'm acting completely in character. The unsuspecting, foolish wife who, assuming her life was perfect, went on television and had the audacity to cry in public. I wish I really was playing the part… in light of what we know now… I really wish. But it's me. All me. What you see is what you get. So. I suppose we got what we wanted. Exactly what we were asking for.

The DETECTIVE*'s phone rings again.*

You'd better get that.

18. ONE WEEK BEFORE

AMY *and* MICHAEL.

AMY: So a Range Rover does about 20 miles per gallon.

MICHAEL: Does it?

AMY: And the Prius, about 50.

MICHAEL: What's that in kilometres per litre?

AMY: They don't measure it like that. Given the average kilometres driven a year, at an average fuel price of $1.30 per litre (and that's cheap now) —that's about a $2,500 saving every year. The hybrids last just as long. They're easier to park. And they're quiet.

MICHAEL: For the silent getaway.

AMY: Total stealth. If you need it.

MICHAEL: They're not very fast.

AMY: They've got excellent acceleration actually. From zero to 60. Because it's electric, it's like flicking the switch on a blender, it responds straight away.

MICHAEL: What about 60 to 100?

AMY: Come on, Dad—let's face it—when do you ever go off-roading?

MICHAEL: You never know when I might have to.

AMY: That's bullshit, Dad. You drive it to the airport and back. That's it.

MICHAEL: I'm not getting out if this / am I?

AMY: No.

MICHAEL: The Prius—it's such an ugly car, Amy.

AMY: How many of your friends drive a Prius?

MICHAEL: None.

AMY: How many of your work colleagues drive a Prius?

MICHAEL: None.

AMY: How many drive a black Range Rover or Porsche or some other ugly, guzzling, global-warmer?

MICHAEL: I don't know…

AMY: At a guess.

MICHAEL: A few.

AMY: Come on, how many do you see parked around the gym on Saturday?

MICHAEL: Not all of them are black.

Okay.

Look, Amy, I like the Range Rover. There's a lot of things we have because we want them, not because we need them. I know what you want me to say. I can hear all your arguments. *Even if you're sceptical, why don't you just act as if it's a reality. There's no harm in playing it safe.* You think I'm scared of what others will think about me so I stick with the status quo.

AMY: You're toying with my future, Dad.

MICHAEL: The Pious. That's what we call them. For people who can afford to say they're doing something about the environment… who want to tell everyone how committed they are… while trying to make everyone else feel guilty.

AMY: It does make a difference and if you can afford it—

MICHAEL: What do you want me to say then?

AMY: I don't want you to say anything. I want you to do it.

Pause.

Can I tell you something?

MICHAEL: Yes.
AMY: You promise not to tell anyone.
MICHAEL: I promise.

>*Pause.*

AMY: I'm a virgin.

>*Slight pause.*

MICHAEL: You don't know how happy that makes me.
AMY: Well, I'm not happy about it.
MICHAEL: A Prius among a whole lot of black Range Rovers.
AMY: Exactly.

19. FIVE DAYS AFTER

ANNE *and the* DETECTIVE, *who is on the phone.*

DETECTIVE: (Yep. Uh-huh. Yep, I'm here now. What? Uh-huh. Where? Jesus. Where's that? Right. Okay. And you've spoken to the dealer? Okay. Okay.)
ANNE: Amy, can you come down here please?
AMY!
AMY: Coming.

>AMY *enters.*

DETECTIVE: (Right. Give me the address. I'm with her. Uh-huh. Fire away. 135. Uh-huh. View Street. Got it. I will. Uh-huh.)

>*He hangs up.*

135 View Street. Sutherland. Do you know anyone who lives there, Anne? Have you ever been to that address?
ANNE: No I haven't.
DETECTIVE: Amy, do you know anything about that address?
ANNE: Why would she?
DETECTIVE: Seen it written down?
AMY: No.
ANNE: Detective.
DETECTIVE: Heard your parents talk about it?
AMY: No.
ANNE: This is completely inappropriate.

AMY: What's going on, Mum?

DETECTIVE: You said your husband drives a Range Rover.

ANNE: That's right, a black one. Plate number SCW509. That's right, isn't it, Amy?

AMY: Yes.

DETECTIVE: That was a call from Detective Sergeant Stephens who you've met. He's located another vehicle registered in your husband's name.

ANNE: Where?

DETECTIVE: In the bushes near Nattai.

ANNE: Nattai? I don't even know where Nattai is.

DETECTIVE: Past Camden.

ANNE: Dumped?

DETECTIVE: We believe so. But it's not a black Range Rover.

ANNE: What is it?

DETECTIVE: A Prius.

ANNE: My husband doesn't drive a Prius.

DETECTIVE: He might not drive a Prius, but he owns one.

ANNE: You saw the registration papers, he owns and drives a black Range Rover.

DETECTIVE: In the front of the Prius, Anne, was a newspaper. Written on it is an address, 135 View Street Sutherland. Who lives there?

ANNE: Quite obviously no-one we know.

DETECTIVE: Have you ever driven a Prius, Anne?

ANNE: We have never seen or heard of a Prius in this house, detective, let alone driven one. So there must be some kind of mistake. Assure the detective what sort of car your father drives, Amy, tell him.

DETECTIVE: We just need to know what's going on, Anne?

ANNE: Amy. Tell him.

JESUS, AMY!

20. FIFTEEN MINUTES AFTER

GARY, *holding a wallet, and* PAULA.

GARY: Well, his name's not Ray fucking Wimple.

PAULA: We knew that much, Gary.

GARY: Michael Devine.

PAULA: I'll look him up.

GARY: See if there's a photo of him.

PAULA: How do you spell Devine?

GARY: D.E. / V...

PAULA: V.I.N.E.

GARY: N.E. Yep.

PAULA: See if there's some business cards or something.

GARY: Here—Michael Devine. 'In Essence'. Bespoke Homes. Look it up.

PAULA: What does he do?

GARY: C.E.O.

PAULA: Jesus. Here it is. Okay, here's a photo of him.

GARY: That's him.

PAULA: This is not good.

GARY: What do you mean?

PAULA: Jesus, Gary, he's fucking rich.

GARY: How rich?

PAULA: I don't know. He's selling places all over the world. Abu Dhabi. Jakarta. Shopping malls in Newcastle.

GARY: We didn't know who he was.

PAULA: Are they going to believe that?

GARY: This's got nothing to do with the money. He's got 100 bucks in here.

PAULA: We got him out of a swingers' mag.

GARY: That's not our fault.

PAULA: You're not listening to me.

GARY: We stick to the story.

PAULA: Self-protection?

GARY: Yeah.

PAULA: What about the bit of the story where they ask us how we afforded all this stuff... how much you've made doing those recons while you've been collecting the dole, Gary. And the media. You see this shit on TV all the time. We laugh at it. But it's us. You're rorting the system. I'm a cleaner who's lost her kids, trying to get her life on track. Then we kill a millionaire. Think about that part of the story.

GARY: Fuck.

PAULA: Yes 'Fuck', Gary.

>*Her phone rings again.*

Jenny again. What time is it? Ohhhhh.

>GARY *is gesturing to answer it.*

Shit, Jenny, I was just about to call you.
Yeah. Gary's chucking up in the bathroom.
It's pretty bad, yeah, but he'll be alright.
Some chicken we reckon.
I'm getting out the door now. I'm so sorry.
Thanks, Jenny. I owe you one.
I will. Thanks.
See you in a bit.

>*She hangs up.*

GARY: Maybe I did murder him, Paula? Did I murder him? At the time I was thinkin'… when he did that to you… I was thinkin'… I did wanta kill him. I did. Where's this woman… his wife or… this girl in the photos he was sending to us? He makes so much money he could've brought a whole fucking brothel for himself. What's he doing here? Jesus. Our story holds up, doesn't it? Listen to me. I don't even know who I am anymore. I mean… what's just happened? We've got a dead millionaire in the bathroom. And we're talking like this. Tell me you're going to work, you'll come home and when I wake up this hasn't happened. I'm serious. Because I can't do this.

PAULA: Gary.

GARY: I mean it.

PAULA: Jesus. My kids are coming back, Gary. Next fucking week. We know what the truth is but…

GARY: That's not gonna save us—

>*The phone rings offstage.*

PAULA: Is that another phone?

GARY: It is. That's his again. I can't go / in there.

PAULA: Alright. Alright. One fucking second.

>PAULA *runs offstage.*

21. ONE WEEK BEFORE

AMY *and* MICHAEL. *His phone rings.*

AMY: Are you going to take that?
MICHAEL: No.

He silences the phone again.

AMY: You don't judge me.
MICHAEL: What for?
AMY: I mean… I know. I'm not exactly the easiest at the moment… I know that.
MICHAEL: Never.
AMY: I probably deserve what I get half the time.
MICHAEL: No. Never. You must never think like that, Amy. Listen to me. I'm your father. And I know what you've said about laying it down… but this is what I'm saying now. No matter what, I'm here. Okay. No matter what happens between us. No matter what I see… the mistakes—the adventures, let's call them adventures—I will not forsake you. I'm not going anywhere. I have a high elasticity. Do you understand that? I don't break easily. It's not that I judge you. I don't think you're this or that. I trust you'll make the right decisions. That we've given you something. You're going to be a great doctor. I know. And yes—yes—I'm proud of that—
AMY: But not the photo.
MICHAEL: It's not your best moment. No. Because one day… one day, Amy…
AMY: Dad.
MICHAEL: I'm sorry.
AMY: No… what?
MICHAEL: One day—you're right—one day I won't be here anymore. And I don't mind dying. It's not that—
AMY: Everybody dies.
MICHAEL: It's the thought that I won't see you again. You. So if something happened to you… suddenly… it'd be more like I was dead. The world would be colourless.
AMY: Well… you can't deny I'm colourful.
MICHAEL: And I don't want to destroy that.

Believe me.

Pause.

AMY: I love you, Michael.

MICHAEL: I love you, Amy.

And what about him… this guy you're sending love letters to.

AMY: Da-ad.

MICHAEL: Do you love him?

22. ONE MONTH AFTER

ANNE *and* PSYCHIATRIST.

PSYCHIATRIST: I'm just wondering. Have you ever seen the place?

ANNE: I have actually. I went there. Is that strange?

PSYCHIATRIST: I might want to see it too. And did that help… to make it more real?

ANNE: My God, the house… I don't know. There's no fence out the front. It's one of those yellow-brick things in the middle of a block. No architectural flair. No flowers. Not even a rose. Just a scrappy, overgrown lawn, with a letterbox in it. A Colorbond fence around the backyard. The sort of house a child draws. There's a line of brick pavers across the lawn from the footpath to the door. But… you know I couldn't walk down it. I did peer through a window… between the curtains. I expected to see… well, I don't know what I expected to see. But not a room… a room like this one.

I looked over the back fence too. The yard was still full of cars. Old chassis and parts strewn around, tyres, shovels—junk. Well, I'd call it junk. He was living off it. They'd filled in the hole… you know. It's funny… I couldn't see Michael there at all. Does that make any sense? I mean… what was he looking for? That he couldn't get from me.

I know it's true that Michael went there… that's where he was… But I don't see it. Like he's not dead. Like someone else died and Michael's missing. He's still missing.

23. THE MORNING OF

JULIA *and* DAVID.

JULIA: What else do you hate, David? Do you hate me?

Pause.

DAVID: No. I don't hate / you.

JULIA: What the fuck is it then? Because you've just about lost me. There was a woman in intensive care last week—

DAVID: Oh, please. No. Don't give me one of these / stories—

JULIA: A woman younger / than me.

DAVID: No no… / no no no.

JULIA: Her two-year-old daughter was sitting by her bed, wondering if she'd wake up. Talking to her mother, like she could hear every word. I don't have enough time. I can't go on if I know you're not with me, if you're going to sabotage everything. I am what I am. And this is what I want. With you. So if it's not with you, let me know please. So I can find someone else. Because right now you're not here, you're somewhere else.

DAVID: Jesus, did you actually listen to what he was saying?

JULIA: It's a sell. He believes in what he sells. So what?

DAVID: That's the problem.

JULIA: Take it or leave it, David. It's an offer. If we like it, we can take it. / Simple as that.

DAVID: Something's…

He gestures to his head.

JULIA: What?

DAVID: There's a gap. I used to see things… like a television. Turn it on. Sit in front of it. Watch something. Point my finger. Talk back to it. Think about getting a new one. But I don't see a television anymore… a couch. I just see worthless shit. Objects I want to smash! See if I'll miss them. If they've actually got any real value. You know. Join the riots. Smash some shops. Loot a few luxury items. Look at him, he's lost his mind? But I haven't. I'm testing things… the limits… I don't know… of sanity. [*He laughs.*] That's stupid. I can hear that. Testing the limits… fuck. So don't roll your eyes at me. It might look like I'm sabotaging but I'm just trying to make it fit. There's something that won't CLICK IN. The shapes won't go through their old holes. You know… Ah ah ah ah ah ah! I am not what I am. You see a life and I see white walls. I'm looking,

Julia... looking for something... the essence of this thing we we're being sold... that's advertised... but I never actually receive. You see: this. This is not it. Not it at all. What if I wake up and find myself trapped... trapped inside the set? I might kill something.

JULIA: Why don't you?!

DAVID: What?

JULIA: Kill something.

Go on.

Be honest with yourself for once in this whole fucking mess.

Go on. Kill it!

DAVID: AH AH AH AH AH AH AH AH AH AH AH!

> DAVID *strips down to his underwear and sits in the middle of the room, defeated.*
>
> *She goes to him.*

JULIA: David. Darling.

DAVID: I'm not your darling David. Don't patronise me, for fuck's sake.

> *Pause.*

JULIA: It was a shock, what happened. No-one expects to be in your position... suddenly out like that. I suppose I'm lucky. People still get sick. That's not going to change.

> MICHAEL *enters.*

MICHAEL: So, what are you two dreaming up?

> MICHAEL*'s phone rings and another phone rings offstage again.*
>
> *He looks at his phone.*
>
> *They all stop and listen.*

24. TWENTY MINUTES AFTER

PAULA *enters with two mobiles. She silences the one that's ringing.*

MICHAEL*'s phone is ringing at the same time. He silences it.*

PAULA: He's running two mobiles. Get my phone and ring the number he called me on.

> GARY *does it.*

Right. [*Holding one mobile up*] This is the number he called us from. We're listed as 'Others'. That's how he covers his tracks.

[*Holding up the other phone*] This is the phone that was ringing before. Missed calls from—Anne. His wife, I bet. Wondering where he is. She's got no fucking clue he's here. So... Michael Devine's missing. Everyone'll be looking for him. But he's not here. He's never been here. Michael Devine's vanished. Alright. And no-one's gonna miss Ray Wimple. No-one knows he even exists—except us. Apart from that he's not real. So let's forget about him.

Listen to me. We deal with it, Gary. On our own. We deal with it.

I'll go to work. As soon as it gets dark you go out 'n' dig a hole. Dig it fucking quietly. Even if it takes you all night. Okay. No-one's gonna hear you or see you. Do it between the red and silver shit-boxes out the back. Okay.

GARY: What are you going to do?

PAULA: Go to work. Come home. Deal with the corpse.

GARY: What about the Prius?

PAULA: We'll dump it tomorrow.

Then we carry on like normal. You do those last two recons. Clean up the fucking yard. The girls come back. You call Mitch and pour some fucking concrete. We do up the bathroom. That's it.

Get Joey and lock him in the laundry.

Give him something to eat.

She kisses him.

GARY: I love you, Paula.

PAULA: See you when I get home.

She leaves.

25. ONE MONTH AFTER

ANNE *and her* PSYCHIATRIST.

ANNE: I got a call, on the street just before.

PSYCHIATRIST: Who from?

ANNE: Lauren Cleary.

PSYCHIATRIST: A friend?

ANNE: Huh. No. She's the woman my husband was having an affair with.

I don't know if I have any friends anymore.

PSYCHIATRIST: No-one?

ANNE: Friends have become a bit of a nightmare. And streets. I'm terrified of seeing people I know… of being recognised. People I haven't seen since.

PSYCHIATRIST: Are you having any nightmares?

ANNE: I am. One actually. It's funny because…

In the dream I get this text message from Michael. He reminds me about a moment when we first met. In my old flat before we moved in together. Thinking about it's turning him on. He comes over, knocks, I open the door, nervous as a schoolgirl.

Are you alone?

Yes, I'm alone.

He tears my clothes off and we're having sex. Then there's another knock on the door. I go and see who it is. I'm looking through the peephole and it's another man, a stranger. He starts yelling, 'Open up, Anne! It's me! You have to wake up!' I look back. Michael's still thrusting… like I'm there. The stranger's knocking and yelling, 'Wake up. Wake up, Anne!' I open the door and the walls vanish. Then there's this crowd of people. And the stranger's still there. Staring at me. People are whispering, 'Who is she? Who the fuck is that woman?'

   Pause.

PSYCHIATRIST: So what happened when Lauren called?

ANNE: She said she'd been meaning to call me for ages. And I'm thinking, not now, please. Anyway, she's apologising and it pops into my head—the two of them in a hotel room somewhere… in Singapore, 'on business'… having sex… Michael in front of a mirror… thrusting. And I burst into tears. I'm hysterical. I can feel it… people staring at me. I'm completely stripped bare. And the world finds nothing sacred in a person stripped bare… bawling in the middle of the street. They don't rush to help you. They walk around. But one man did, a stranger. 'Are you okay?'

'No, I'm not okay. Does it fucking look like I'm okay? You fucking idiot. Fuck off. Fuck off, will you?'

Maybe that's what it is… what it was all along… a charade.

PSYCHIATRIST: What's that?

ANNE: Our dignity. A charade. Because I have this fury in me... you see... but he's gone. He's not here. And I have this urge to...

PSYCHIATRIST: What, Anne? An urge to what?

26. ONE WEEK BEFORE

AMY *and* MICHAEL.

MICHAEL: I'm sorry. You don't have to answer that. Not now. You probably don't even know yet. But if something... anything happens.

AMY: I'll tell you.

MICHAEL: Good. You've got no reason to be scared.

AMY: I know.

MICHAEL: It's love. You're good at it. It suits you.

AMY: Does it?

MICHAEL: It does. I'll promise you something.

AMY: What?

MICHAEL: I will. I'll get a Prius.

27. EIGHT HOURS AFTER

The sound of a saw. It stops. PAULA *enters with a sleeping bag full of body parts, a face mask over her face, bloody shirt, and a jerry can.* GARY *enters with a shovel.*

PAULA: Clean the bathroom. Use my stuff out of the car. I'll come back in a minute and help you.

GARY: Does that have to be in here?

PAULA: I can't exactly stand out the front with it.

GARY: It's ready.

> *A phone rings on the bench.*
>
> *He smashes it.*

PAULA: Give that to me.

> *She puts it in the sleeping bag.*
>
> *They go out.*
>
> *Blackout.*

28. THE MOMENT

PAULA, GARY *and* RAY *offstage.*

PAULA: Gary, don't go out there… / Ohhhh! Jesus, Gary!

> GARY *exits.*

GARY: I'm telling him to fuck off— [*Off*] Just fuck off now, Ray. I mean it. Fuck off.

> *The phone rings again.*

> *The dog keeps barking.*

> PAULA *goes out to attend to the dog again.*

PAULA: [*off*] JOEY. COME HERE. COME HERE, JOEY. YOU LITTLE SHIT.

> *The dog stops barking.*

Good boy.

GARY: [*off*] No I mean it, Ray. Fuck off.

RAY: [*off*] Just one second.

GARY: [*off*] Stay back there.

RAY: [*off*] I'm not going to hurt anyone.

GARY: [*off*] No-one said you were. Stay… get your foot / out… No!

RAY: [*off*] Just let me in to have a quick chat.

GARY: [*off*] No, Ray!

RAY: [*off*] We're all adults. Come on, / Gary.

GARY: [*off*] Fuck you—No!

> RAY *enters the house with a green shopping bag full of grapefruit.*

> GARY *follows after him.*

> RAY *is laughing.*

RAY: So here we are again.

GARY: What do you want, Ray?

RAY: Just a chat.

GARY: Look, this is 'break'n'enta'.

RAY: I don't want to steal anything, Gary.

GARY: Paula, get in here, will you?

RAY: I like Paula much more than Daisy.

He takes out a grapefruit.

PAULA enters.

You got any sugar to put on this. Perfect combination of sweet and sour. Makes your come taste… mmm. Shall we share a bowl before we get started?

GARY: We're not getting started / with anything.

PAULA: What the fuck's he doing in here?

RAY: Hi, Paula. Did you get my text?

PAULA: Fuck off, Ray.

RAY walks up to PAULA and gropes her breast.

RAY: I remember these.

In a reflex she slaps him.

Ohhh! I like it. It's my birthday next week, maybe you can give me an early present: slap me while you ride me.

He moves in to touch her again.

GARY pushes him back.

GARY: That's enough, Ray.

RAY: Hey, Gary, don't be like that, it's your turn now… as soon as she gets here she's all yours. We'll watch while you get your end away this time. Even up the score.

GARY: No, mate, we know she's not coming.

RAY: Ye of such little faith, Gary.

GARY: She doesn't even exist.

RAY: She exists alright… you've seen the photos. How's that gash, Gary? Huh? You remember. Think about it. It's going to be fucking sweet and wet. Come on, Paula. Come over here. Maybe we can get poor Gary in the mood.

RAY starts stripping.

PAULA: What the fuck's / he doing?

GARY: Uh-uh, Ray.

RAY: Cranky mechanic… everyone's in such a bad mood.

GARY: Put it away, mate.

RAY: Must be the heat. A drink… you haven't offered me a drink.

GARY: No drinks. / I mean it.

RAY: I won't try and touch you this time, Gary, I swear. I'll play by / the rules—

GARY: Okay… Just clear outta here before this gets out of hand.

RAY: Come on! We all know what we want. She's turning up any minute. I promise. Just relax. She'll join us when she gets here. Oh yes—

> RAY *starts masturbating quite vigorously.*

PAULA: No, Gary!

RAY: Look, you're wife is gagging for it.

PAULA: Jesus, Gary.

RAY: Time for a quick ride with Daddy on the / couch, Paula.

PAULA: I'm not your little girl.

GARY: Get out of here!

RAY: Surely you old fuck rats are used to this.

PAULA: Get this sick fuck out of here, Gary.

> RAY *keeps masturbating.*

> *The dog starts barking.*

RAY: Ooooo, yes. That's it, come and join / me now, Paula.

GARY: I mean it. Get out of here, Ray!

RAY: See, it's not so bad.

PAULA: GARY!

GARY: Alright. Fucking shut that dog up.

> GARY *grabs a hammer off the table.*

RAY: Hey. Hey.

GARY: You've pushed me too far… / too fucking far.

RAY: HEY! Whow. Hang on a minute, / mate, Gary.

GARY: No hanging on.

RAY: WHOW! There's been a misunderstanding.

GARY: No misunderstandings, mate. It said in the ad: 'a couple'. And you keep turning up by yourself—THAT FUCKING DOG, PAULA, I SWEAR.

> PAULA *goes out.*

RAY: You had to watch last time… it's not fair. I get that.

GARY: You're not getting it—

RAY: You're anxious to even up the score… / I know.

GARY: That's not it.

PAULA: [*off*] Come here. Joey. I mean it. Shut up, Joey.

RAY: I really won't touch your dick this time, Gary—

GARY: No, you won't.

>GARY *moves forward.*

RAY: Hey, put that down, mate.

GARY: You're not going to fuck us around. / Okay.

RAY: No. I'm going.

GARY: We didn't invite you. / And that's it.

RAY: I'm going. Alright.

>*He gets ready to leave.*

Alright. I'm out of here.

>PAULA *comes back in.*

>RAY *turns back.*

So what are you two going to do? Hire another prostitute? Like you said... you can't really afford it. Can you? I come for free... no... better... how about this: I'll give you 100 bucks if you let me fuck her, Gary. You make money.

>GARY *lifts the hammer.*

GARY: My God, Ray, I swear!

PAULA: Gary!

RAY: Fine. Fine.

>*He laughs and goes to leave again.*

(Fucking Neanderthal.)

GARY: What did you say?

RAY: Nothing.

GARY: What did you call me?

>*Slight pause.*

RAY: You're a mechanic... yeah? How did you afford all these improvements?

GARY: None of your business.

RAY: Just wondering. Alright I'm off then.

>*He goes to leave. He turns again.*

Oh. What I said before…
I called you a fucking Neanderthal, Gary.
But you're probably so stupid you don't even know what that is.

> GARY *grabs* RAY.

Let me go. Let me fucking go, / you fuck.

> GARY *drags him back into the room.*

GARY: Get back in here, / you fuck.
PAULA: No. / No, Gary. No.
RAY: You fuck. / You fucking fucker. Let me go.

> GARY *hits him on the hand with the hammer.*

> RAY *screams.*

PAULA: Gary!

> *He continues to groan and whimper.*

GARY: Explain that to your wife.
PAULA: What's going on?
GARY: This piece of shit has an apology to make to you.
PAULA: What did you do to him?
GARY: Doesn't matter. As soon as he makes an apology, I'm gonna let him go. So, Ray, I'd like you to apologise to my wife here for what you just did on her couch. Okay. Now up you come!

> *He lifts him to face her.*

Face to face. Like a real man.
PAULA: Just throw him out, Gary.
GARY: As soon as he apologises, Paula. Then he's on his way. Come over here, Paula. So he can talk to you.

> *She takes a few steps forward.*

Okay. It's up to you now, Ray. When you're ready.

> *Long pause.*

RAY: Fat fucking slag.

> *He spits on her.*

GARY: You fucker!

> GARY *raises the hammer.*

PAULA: GARY!

> *The dog stops barking.*
>
> *Blackout.*

29. ONE MONTH AFTER

Night. ANNE *is alone in the dark.* AMY *enters.*

AMY: Jesus. Mum. Turn on a light.

ANNE: I'm fine.

AMY: Okay. Weirdo.

> *Long pause.*

Are you waiting for someone?

ANNE: Yes.

AMY: Who?

ANNE: You.

AMY: This house is getting stranger.

ANNE: I don't know about the house. But your mother is strange. You have a strange mother.

AMY: My friends would love you. They love 'strange'. I'm not strange enough. I'll have to keep you away from the guys. They all think you're hot. If they know you're strange too, they'll throw themselves at you.

ANNE: How do you know that?

AMY: They tell me.

ANNE: They talk to you… like that?

AMY: They fantasise about you. They say we're a 'gifted family'.

ANNE: In looks you mean?

AMY: Yep.

ANNE: I'd agree with that.

AMY: Are you flattered?

ANNE: No.

AMY: You are.

ANNE: You're drunk.

AMY: I might be.

ANNE: How was the party?

AMY: Boozy but boring. It was a boring party. There were no guys.

ANNE: None?

AMY: There was one. But he told me how hot he thought you were and I kinda lost interest.

Michelle, Katie and I decided we want to go to on a trip.

ANNE: Where?

AMY: We were looking at photos of Koh Samui.

ANNE: I hate Koh Samui. It's awful. Wouldn't go to Asia if you paid me.

AMY: Luckily you don't have to go.

Are you drunk?

ANNE: I couldn't sleep.

AMY: Did you go out tonight?

ANNE: I can't go out.

AMY: You should really try and get out, Mum.

So what is it?

ANNE: I collapsed eight months into my pregnancy with you, with heart failure.

AMY: I know. You've told me this a million times.

ANNE: No I haven't.

AMY: Every birthday. Why I'm an only a child. Dad loved telling it actually.

ANNE: He did.

AMY: They had to resuscitate you… took them 70 minutes. Normally they'd only do 20 minutes if you weren't responding… you know… then you went into a coma for a few days after that. The story about how we both survived.

ANNE: No-one gave me much of a chance, not after 70 minutes. Even if I did make it back they thought I'd be 'damaged'.

AMY: But you sprung back to life.

ANNE: Completely *compos mentis*.

I could've had children again.

AMY: No-one blames you, Mum.

ANNE: But I didn't, because it took a long time for me to want to be your mother. To be able to hold you… you know, really hold you again. Do you know what I remember from that time? In the coma?

AMY: No.

ANNE: Nothing.

You hear the stories. People leaving their body. The white lights and fucking tunnels. Hovering over your self, making the decision whether to be reunited with life or not... Oh God, I mean... the life-changing experience. They write their books. 'On the divinity of existence'. And people actually ask me, intelligent people: 'Well... was there something?—did you see anything?' Nothing. I experienced nothing. No lights, darkness, out-of-body experiences. Nothing.

Apparently I looked quite beautiful lying there. Like a china doll. That's what your father said. He sat for hours. Not sleeping. Keeping 'vigil'. Always positive. Ever faithful. Until I woke. We went on with our life, raising you. And I said nothing about it. Kept it hidden. But it's always there. Stretching on in my mind... just below the surface. Flat oblivion. And you know, Amy... I'm terrified that I'm still stranded there. I see it. Not alone at night... No. At traffic lights... you know. Or waiting for a teller machine... in the shower. When I look at you. You see. When I look at you. It terrifies me.

A slight pause.

Huh. But really... I wouldn't even know if I was actually there. Would I?

Silence.

Blackout.

THE END

Griffin Theatre Company presents the World Premiere of

DREAMS IN WHITE
BY DUNCAN GRAHAM

SBW Stables Theatre
8 February – 23 March
Dreams in White was first performed at the SBW
Stables Theatre, Sydney, 13 February 2013

Director
Tanya Goldberg

Designer
Teresa Negroponte

Lighting Designer
Hartley T A Kemp

Composer
Kelly Ryall

Dramaturg
Tessa Leong

Stage Manager
Edwina Guinness

Fight Choreographer
Scott Witt

Production Intern
Rebecca Blake

With
Lucy Bell, Mandy McElhinney,
Andrew McFarlane, Steve Rodgers,
Sara West

G T C
R H O
I E M
F A P
F T A
I R N
N E Y

Australian Government | Australia Council for the Arts | NSW GOVERNMENT Trade & Investment Arts NSW

PLAYWRIGHT'S NOTE

We live in a society of spectacle. At the point of creation, products, events and identities simultaneously become images.

Put in circulation – by marketing or the mechanisms of security – these images have capital. And we willingly participate. Politicians open their bedrooms. Theatres open their rehearsals. Police weapons are fitted with cameras. Citizens post photos of their intimacies. Which part of our lives will not be made available for spectacle?

"We've become our own representatives in a strange commerce, guarantors of a personalization that...feels...like an amputation" (The Invisible Committee). The private is emptied in a farce of verisimilitude.

Where can the 'individual' reclaim their privacy? In another, more secret identity? Or its total annihilation?

The spectacle also opens a search for authenticity – the genuine, real, appropriate mode of human life. We ask: what really happened; how we really felt; who we really are. Authenticity grants authority; and authority demands its legitimate representation – evidenced in the politics of refugees.

Film, theatre, television and photographs are instruments for authoritative representation. Yet in every 'true' exposition lurks a divide – political, racial, economic – between the proper and improper, the included and excluded. Shame and arrogance, conformity and marginality are the poles of this experience.

Dreams in White is based on 'real-life' events but never authentically re-presents them. It attempts to collide the included and excluded; and release the terror and violence contained within.

Snowtown, and other 'true-crime' stories, are often praised for their 'authenticity'. They bring to life the 'chilling brutality' of the socially excluded. "Yet we are safe in the knowledge that this 'authentic' experience is far removed from our own—that 'authenticity' lies in forgotten communities...far removed from the...cinemas [and theatres] where we look on in dismay" (Rebecca Harkins-Cross).

In our portrayal of the middle class, we are often more diligent in our search for authenticity, confirming the class desire to be acknowledged, hold up the mirror and know ourselves. In such a theatre the situations, characters and foibles are "acceptable to the people who have the inclination and the disposable income to attend the theatre:...the liberal middle class" (Daniel Keene).

What if authenticity is to theatre what photography is to painting? A reason to abandon the quest for true representation, and "remake the violence of reality itself" (Francis Bacon).

I'm in search for volatility: a poetic and political theatre that allows the darkness outside the edges of authenticity to disturb our view. To shatter the mirror.

Duncan Graham

DIRECTOR'S NOTE

A frantic couple, a father and teenage daughter's late night heart-to-heart, a haunted widow, a burnt-out professional and a glossy show home. Between our private selves and what we show the world lies a universe of desires, of dreams.

Duncan's play, with its vivid characters and familiar-but-different worlds had me hooked from the first pages of my first read. It fired my director's imagination and satisfied my reader's appetite, quickly revealing itself to be a whole lot more than just a great page-turner.

Dreams in White is an intimate investigation of shame and yearning, connection and disconnection. It delicately, intimately interrogates the self we know, the one we think we know and the one we'd prefer no one else knew.

This compartmentalisation of lives frames bigger questions of wealth, class and power and also makes for great theatre. For me it is the very heart of the play: that prickly, dangerous space that buzzes with the tension between our insides and outsides, between what we let out and keep within. Are our actions for purpose or for show? And who are we showing? Are we trying to manage our perception in the eyes of strangers, for loved ones or for ourselves?

This brave, immediate play is a thriller and a meditation, a question and a proposition, a dream-fiction and very, very real.

Tanya Goldberg

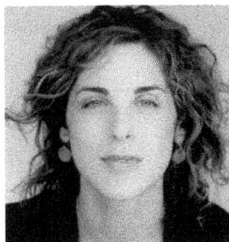

Duncan Graham
Playwright

Duncan graduated as an actor from ACArts, Adelaide, in 2003. His first play, *Black Crow Lullabies*, was the recipient of the 2006 Adelaide Fringe Award for Best New Work. In 2008 he won the Jill Blewett Playwright's Award and was shortlisted for the award in 2006, 2010 and 2012. He was recently shortlisted for the 2011 Griffin Award with *Wolf Hunger*; and for the 2012 Max Afford Playwrights' Award for *Dreams in White*. His work has been commissioned and produced across the country by Belvoir, STC, Malthouse Theatre and STCSA, as well as his own independent company floogle. In 2012 Duncan was a member of the 2012 Griffin Studio and a PWA Associate with Sydney Theatre Company.

Tanya Goldberg
Director

As co-artistic director of independent theatre company Ride On Theatre, Tanya's directing includes: *The Blind Date Project* (Sydney Festival and Brisbane Powerhouse), *The Story of Mary MacLane By Herself* (Griffin Theatre Company, Malthouse Theatre and Merrigong Theatre), *Way To Heaven* (Griffin Independent), *An Oak Tree*, *Merchant of Venice & Loveplay* (all BSharp), and *Debris* (Tamarama Rock Surfers). **Other directing:** *Lovely Ugly* (Griffin Theatre Company Studio), *Der Gelbe Stern* (Adelaide & Melbourne Cabaret Festivals, Seymour Centre), *The Crucible* (STC), *Macbeth* (WAAPA), *Sparkleshark* (NIDA), *The Girl on the Sofa* (New Theatre). **Assistant directing includes:** *American Document* (SITI Company & Martha Graham Dance Co, NYC), *War of the Roses* (STC), Gate Theatre Dublin's Sydney Festival Beckett season of *First Love*, *Eh Joe* and *I'll Go On*; and *L'Orfeo* (Pinchgut Opera). Tanya has received several international fellowships to work with some of the world's leading theatremakers in

New York, Germany, and Chicago, and was a member of the 2012 Griffin Studio. Tanya directed the award-winning short films *Great Western*, funded by Screen NSW's Emerging Filmmaker Fund, and *Heck*, and is the producer on the short film *Pig*, which screened in Official Selection at both the Berlinale and Cannes Cinema des Antipodes, 2011.

Tessa Leong
Assistant Director

Tessa is the director and founding member of theatre company isthisyours? and works on an ongoing basis with artists for The Australian Bureau of Worthiness. Her work over the past six years with companies across the country as a director and assistant director have fed her love of new and challenging work. Tessa is part of the 2013 Griffin Studio.

Tess Negroponte
Designer

Teresa Negroponte graduated from NIDA in 2009 and was the recipient of the 2010 NIDA/Sydney Grammar School Fellowship. She has designed costumes for a handful of short films in Sydney, has worked as wardrobe stylist for the ABC and Seven Network, and designed a number of sets and costumes for theatre companies including Downstairs Belvoir, Darlinghurst Theatre Company, and recently, the costumes for Boundary St, Black Swan State Theatre Company's inaugural production at the new Heath Ledger Theatre at the Perth International Arts Festival, and the 2012 Brisbane Festival. She also designed the costumes for Dr. Zhivago, the new musical produced by the Gordon Frost Organisation, which opened in Sydney and toured to Melbourne, Brisbane and Korea. Teresa is currently designing the costumes for a new production of *Tosca* directed by John Bell for Opera Australia.

Hartley T A Kemp
Lighting Designer

Australian theatre includes *Les Liaisons Dangereuses* and *In the Next Room*, or the *Vibrator Play* (STC), *Old Man* (Belvoir); *Duchess of Malfi* (Bell Shakespeare), *Rapid Write – Hollywood Ending* (Arts Radar/Theatre503/Griffin), T*he Story of Mary MacLane by Herself* (Ride On Theatre/ Malthouse/Griffin), *The Gift* (MTC), *Cordelia* (Little Dove

Theatre Art/Motherboard). Recent international work includes: *A Number* (Fugard, Cape Town) and *A Little Night Music on Broadway*. Recent UK work includes: *Sunset Baby* (Gate), *Our New Girl* (Bush), *Love, Love, Love* (Paines Plough) and *Lower Ninth* (Donmar). In London Hartley has lit productions for the National Theatre, Royal Shakespeare Company, Old Vic, Royal Court, Donmar Warehouse, Almeida, Gate, Lyric Hammersmith, Hampstead Theatre, Menier Chocolate Factory, Opera Holland Park, Southwark Playhouse, ROH Linbury Studio, Theatre Royal Stratford East, Tricycle, and the West End. UK regional work includes productions for Birmingham Rep, Bristol Old Vic, Castleward Opera, Chichester Festival Theatre, Clwyd Teatr Cymru, Exeter Northcott, Manchester Royal Exchange, Sheffield Theatres and West Yorkshire Playhouse. In Europe Hartley has lit for the Gate Theatre Dublin, English Theatre Frankfurt, Tiroler Landesteater Innsbruck and Gothenburg Opera. Hartley is artistic director of C venues at the Edinburgh Festival Fringe.

Kelly Ryall
Composer

Kelly Ryall is an award winning composer and sound artist. In 2009 he received 2 Green Room awards for *Love Monkey* and *Coop*, in 2007 he received the Melbourne International Arts Festival Award and in 2005 received a Green Room Award and Fringe Festival Award for outstanding composition and sound design. His recent works include: *The School for Wives* (Bell Shakespeare), *On the Misconception of Oedipus* (Malthouse, PTC), *Macbeth* (Bell Shakespeare), *On the Production of Monsters* (MTC), *Disappearing Acts* (World Theatre Festival), *The Boys* (Griffin/Sydney Festival), *Return To Earth* (MTC), And *No More Shall We Part* (Griffin Theatre Company), *Julius Caesar* (Bell Shakespeare), *Die Winterreise* (Thin Ice, Malthouse), Sundowner (KAGE), *Save For Crying* (Angus Cerini/Doubletap), *Expectation* (Arts House), *The Trial* (Malthouse, Sydney Theatre Co, Thin Ice), *Dead Man's Cell Phone* (MTC), *Love Me Tender* (Company B, Griffin and Thin Ice), *The Harry Harlow Project* (Full Tilt), *The Man With The September Face* (Full Tilt), *God Of Carnage* (MTC) and *One Night The Moon* (Malthouse).

Lucy Bell
Performer

Lucy has performed extensively on stage including productions of *The Cherry Orchard*, *As You Like It* and *Darling Oscar* for the Sydney Theatre Company; *Speaking In Tongues*, *Through The Wire*, *The Falls* and *Wolf Lullaby* for Griffin Theatre Company; *Twelfth Night* and *Blue Murder* for Belvoir; *The Duchess of Malfi*, *Pericles* and *Twelfth Night* for Bell Shakespeare; and *For Julia* for the Melbourne Theatre Company. Recent feature film credits include *The Square* and *Ten Empty*. On television, Lucy has appeared in *30 Seconds*, *City Homicide*, *Wildside*, *Dirt Game*, *Bastard Boys*, *Farscape*, *All Saints*, *Grass Roots*, *My Husband, My Killer*, *Murder Call* and ABC's *Crownies*. In 2013, Lucy will be seen in the ABC telemovie *Magazine Wars*.

Mandy McElhinney
Performer

Mandy has recently received a nomination for the 2012 AACTA Awards for Best Guest or Supporting Actress in a Television Drama for her role in *Howzat: Kerry Packer's War*. In 2010 she was nominated for the USA Helen Hayes Award for Outstanding Supporting Performer in a Play for Sydney Theatre Company's *A Streetcar Named Desire* in Washington DC. In 1998 she was nominated for a Green Room Award for Best Actress in a featured role for *The Herbal Bed* at Melbourne Theatre Company. She has appeared in numerous television series including *MDA*, *All Saints*, *The Alice*, *Bed of Roses*, *Kath & Kim* and 4 consecutive series of Comedy Inc. More recently Mandy has appeared in *A Moody Christmas* and will be seen in the upcoming ABC telemovie *Magazine Wars*. She has appeared in the feature film *The Bank*. Theatre roles include Sydney Theatre Company credits include *The Beauty Queen of Leenane*, *In the Next Room or The Vibrator Play*, *The Great*, *Don's Party* and Kafka's *Metamorphosis*. For Melbourne Theatre Company Mandy has appeared in *The Hypocrite*, *Don's Party*, *Life After George* and *Pride & Prejudice*. For Playbox Theatre, she has appeared in *This Way Up*, *Holy Day* and *Inside 2000*. *Dreams in White* will be Mandy's first show with Griffin Theatre Company. Mandy has been a proud member of MEAA for over twenty years.

Andrew McFarlane
Performer

Andrew is a graduate of NIDA, and has had an extensive career in film, television and theatre. He has starred in some of Australia's most successful TV dramas including *The Sullivans*, *Patrol Boat*, *The Flying Doctors*, *Water Rats*, *Blue Heelers*, *The Alice*, and *Underbelly: A Tale of Two Cities* and numerous telemovies and mini-series. Andrew has worked for every state theatre company in Australia and for numerous independent and commercial theatre companies. His credits include George in *Who's Afraid of Virginia Woolf*, Salieri in *Amadeus* and Bernard Nightingale in *Arcadia*. He has performed in seven David Williamson plays (four of which were premieres of new works) and most recently appeared for Melbourne Theatre Company in *The Heretic* and in the Toby Schmitz play *I Want To Sleep with Tom Stoppard* for Tamarama Rock Surfers. He is a course director at the Darlinghurst Theatre School and is also a regular presenter on Play School for the ABC.

Steve Rodgers
Performer

Steve trained as an actor at Theatre Nepean. His stage credits include: *That Eye The Sky* for Burning House Theatre; *Last Cab to Darwin* for Pork Chop Productions; *Three Sisters*, *She Stoops to Conquer*, *The Comedy of Errors*, *As You Like It*, *Democracy*, *The Miser* and *Riflemind* for Sydney Theatre Company; *The Boys Next Door*, *All My Sons*, *Lobby Hero*, *A Streetcar Named Desire*, *Diving for Pearls* and *Humble Boy* for Ensemble Theatre; *A Midsummer Night's Dream* and *Macbeth* for Bell Shakespeare Company; *The Pillow Man*, *Twelfth Night*, *Night on Bald Mountain*, *Cloudstreet*, *The Blind Giant is Dancing*, *Measure For Measure* and *The Kiss* for Belvoir. Steve has worked with some of Australia's best screen directors, having appeared in films such as *The Men's Group*, *Bitter and Twisted*, *The Money*, *You Can't Stop the Murders*, *The Bank*, *La Spagnola*, *Oscar and Lucinda*, *Dead Heart* and *Children of the Revolution*. His television credits are many, most recently appearing in *Devils Dust* and as Alan Bond in the ABC series *Paper Giants 2: Magazine Wars*. As a writer Steve's first full-length play, *Ray's Tempest*, was short listed for the Patrick White Playwrights' award, nominated for Best

New Australian Work for the Sydney Theatre Awards and received two main-stage productions at Belvoir and the Melbourne Theatre Company. He then wrote *Savage River* which was developed by PlayWriting Australia and nominated for Best New Australian Work for the Sydney Theatre Awards. It received productions at Griffin Theatre Company, Melbourne Theatre Company and the Tasmanian Theatre Company. His most recent work, *FOOD*, (which he co-directed with Kate Champion of Force Majeure) played at Belvoir in 2012 and has recently been picked up by La Boite and also for a tour of Victoria. It will tour extensively throughout Australia and internationally in 2014. As well as writing for television and mentoring other writers, Steve has been a proud member of MEAA for over twenty years.

Sara West
Performer

Sara graduated with Honours from the Flinders Drama Centre in 2010. Most recently she has wrapped on shooting Nick Matthews' feature film *One Eyed Girl*. Other film credits include shorts *Collision*, *Lily and Sam* and MIFF Australian Short Winner, *Spine*. For theatre, Sara's credits include *Don's Party*, *Love*, *Some Girls* (Flinders Drama Centre); *God is Dead* (Stone/Castro) and *Don't Look Back* (Adelaide Bank Festival of the Arts). In 2012 she made her Sydney stage debut with the well-received Belvoir production, *Babyteeth*.

Edwina Guinness
Stage Manager

Edwina graduated with a Bachelor of Dramatic Art/ Production from the Victorian College of the Arts in 2006. She has worked extensively as both a Stage Manager and an Assistant Stage Manager for companies including the Sydney Theatre Company, Belvoir, Griffin Theatre Company, Bell Shakespeare Company, Malthouse, Melbourne Theatre Company, Victorian Opera and Australian Opera. Shows she has worked on include *The Boys*, *Beautiful One Day*, *Under Milk Wood*, *Bloodland*, *'Tis Pity She's a Whore*, *Just Macbeth*, *The Power of Yes*, *The War of the Roses*, and *Othello*; among many others.

ABOUT GRIFFIN

Griffin Theatre Company is Australia's new writing theatre. In residence at Sydney's historic SBW Stables Theatre, we lead the country in developing and producing great Australian stories, and are dedicated to supporting Australian artists.

Formed in 1978, Griffin took up residence at the SBW Stables Theatre in 1980. For over 30 years since, the Company has been the boutique powerhouse of Australian theatre: consistently breaking new ground and making an outstanding contribution to the national culture.

Griffin has always been the place to make a great start. Australia's most loved and performed play – Michael Gow's *Away* – premiered at Griffin. The hit films *Lantana* and *The Boys* also began life as plays first produced by the company, as did the TV series *Heartbreak High*. Many artists who now contribute significantly to the Australian theatre, film and television industries began professional careers at Griffin, including Cate Blanchett, Jacqueline McKenzie and David Wenham.

In recent years, this success has continued with smash hits like *The Boys, Angela's Kitchen* and *Speaking In Tongues*, and return seasons and national and international tours of plays including *Savage River, The Story of the Miracles at Cookie's Table, Mr Bailey's Minder* and *Holding the Man*.

Now, Griffin is the only professional theatre company in Australia entirely dedicated to the development and production of new Australian plays. Presenting four or five productions each year, Griffin regularly tours across Australia. The company also acts as a hub for artists and audiences alike; co-presenting the best independent theatre in Sydney through Griffin Independent; providing audiences with diverse and innovative experiences through Griffringe and Griffin

Between the Lines; nurturing the theatre-makers of tomorrow through our education program, the Griffin Ambassadors; and harnessing the talents of the country's best emerging writers and directors through our resident artist scheme, the Griffin Studio.

Griffin Theatre Company
13 Craigend St, Kings Cross NSW 2011

Phone 02 9332 1052

Fax 02 9331 1524

Email info@griffintheatre.com.au

Web www.griffintheatre.com.au

SBW Stables Theatre
10 Nimrod St
Kings Cross NSW 2011

Online bookings at griffintheatre.com.au or call 02 9361 3817

URGENT
THEATRICA
GENUINE
PLAYFUL
FARE
MAGICA
INTIM

GRIFFIN STAFF AND DONORS

Patron
Seaborn, Broughton
and Walford Foundation

Griffin acknowledges the generosity
of the Seaborn, Broughton and
Walford Foundation in allowing
it, since 1986, the use of the
SBW Stables Theatre rent free,
less outgoings.

Board
Michael Bradley (Chair),
Hilary Bell, Damian Borchok,
Lee Lewis, Lisa Lewin (Treasurer),
Sophie McCarthy, Kate Mulvany,
Leigh O'Neill and Stuart Thomas

Artistic Director
Lee Lewis

Associate Artist
Jane Bodie

General Manager
Simon Wellington

Deputy General Manager
Viv Rosman

Finance Manager
Alison Baly

Production Managers
Micah Johnson
Jeremy Page

Marketing Manager
Jennifer Cannock

**Digital & Social Media Manager
(maternity leave)**
Stephanie Hui

Publicist
Michael Morcos

Development Manager
Brooke Ravens

**Administration & Program
Coordinator**
Melanie Carolan

Box Office Manager
Brendon Johnson

Front of House Supervisors
Liz Arday, Rebecca Martin
and Luke Rogers

Bar Manager
Damien Storer

Griffin Studio
Angela Betzien, Tessa Leong,
Iain Sinclair, Sue Smith

Affiliate Directors
Lucas Jervies & Pierce Wilcox

Affiliate Writers
Chris Summers & Julian Larnach

Writers Under Commission
Tom Holloway (Tears Run Cold)
Kit Brookman (A Rabbit for
Kim Jong-Il)
Maxine Mellor (The Silver Alps)
Declan Greene

Web Developer
House of Laudanum

Brand and Graphic Design
Interbrand

Cover Photography
Katie Kaars

Income from Griffin activities covers less than 50% of our operating costs – leaving an ever increasing gap for us to fill through government funding sponsorship and the generosity of our individual supporters. Your support helps us bridge the gap and keep ticket prices affordable and our work at its best. To make a donation and a difference, contact Griffin on 9332 1052 or donate online at griffintheatre.com.au.

Commission $12,500+
Darin-Cooper family
Anthony and Suzanne Maple-Brown

Production $10,000+
Anonymous (2)
Estate of the late Ruth Barratt
Sophie McCarthy & Antony Green

Studio $5,000
Gil Appleton
Alex Byrne & Sue Hearn
James Emmett & Peter Wilson
Ros & Paul Espie
Fiona Garrood, Matthew May
& Ayumu Kaneda
The Goodness Foundation
Limb Family Foundation
Richard & Elizabeth Longes
Rhonda McIver
Leigh O'Neill
Geoff & Wendy Simpson
Sam Strong & Katherine Slattery

Workshop $1,000-$4,999
Dr Gae Anderson
Baly Douglass Foundation
Daniel Brezniak
Richard Cottrell
Innes Ferguson
Larry & Tina Grumley
John & Mary Holt
Ken & Lilian Horler
Margaret Johnston
Stephen Manning
Peter & Diane O'Connell
Stuart Thomas
Estate of the late
Leslie N Walford
Paul & Jennifer Winch

Reading $500-$999
Anonymous (3)
Jes Andersen
Wendy Ashton
Jason Bourne
Alex Bowen & Catherine Sullivan
Angela Bowne
Michael & Colleen Chesterman
Wendy Elder
Elizabeth Evatt
Jono Gavin
Peter Graves
Peter & Rosemary Ingle

Alexandra Joel & Philip Mason
Henry Johnston
Dr Stephen McNamara
Dr David Nguyen
Lynne O'Neill
Anthony Paull
Natalie Pelham
Annabel Ritchie
Lesley & Andrew Rosenberg
Isla Tooth
Vodafone Foundation
Louise Walsh & Dave Jordan
Dr Bill Winspear

First Draft $200-$499
Anonymous (4)
Jane Bridge
Katharine Brisbane
Rob Brookman
Corinne Campbell & Bryan Everts
Victor Cohen & Rosie McColl
Bryony & Timothy Cox
Max Dingle
Eric Dole
Peter Fritz
Gadens Lawyers
Julien & Monica Ginsberg
Brenda Gottsche
Janet Heffernan
Danielle Hoareau
Beverley Johnson
Lou Lander
Jennifer Ledgar & Bob Lim
Christopher McCabe
Duncan McKay
Sarah Miller
Neville Mitchell
Philip & Monica Moore
Alex-Oonagh Redmond
Catherine Rothery
Diane & David Russell
Michelle Shek
Ross Steele
Ros Tarszisz

We would also like to thank
Peter O'Connell and Jon Clark
for their expertise, guidance
and time.

Current as of 10 January 2013

GRIFFIN SPONSORS

Griffin would like to thank the following:

Government Supporters

Australian Government | Australia Council for the Arts

NSW GOVERNMENT | Trade & Investment Arts NSW

CITYOFSYDNEY

Patron

SB&W Foundation
SEABORN, BROUGHTON & WALFORD FOUNDATION

2013 Season Sponsor

Interbrand

Production Sponsors

HOLDING REDLICH

nabprivatewealth | nab

Associate Sponsors

MARQUE

tonkin zulaikha greer
ARCHITECTS

OTTO RISTORANTE

BDO

Company Sponsors

WHIRLWIND
More than ink on paper

V & R
THE VICTORIA ROOM
BAR RESTAURANT

EIGHT HOTELS
AUSTRALIA
Boutique Hotel Collection

CURRENCY PRESS

TimeOut
Sydney
timeout.com/sydney

bourke street bakery

Rosenfeld, Kant & Co.
Business & Financial Solutions

SIGNWAVE
NEWTOWN

thewinesociety

REGENTS COURT
UNIQUE STYLISH STUDIO ACCOMMODATION

UNSW
THE UNIVERSITY OF NEW SOUTH WALES

goget
.com.au

Foundations and Trusts

CAL | Cultural Fund

GIRGENSOHN FOUNDATION

ROBERTSON FOUNDATION

Griffin Theatre Company is assisted by the Australian Government through the Australia Council, its arts funding and advisory body; and the NSW Government through Arts NSW.

www.ingramcontent.com/pod-product-compliance
Lightning Source LLC
Chambersburg PA
CBHW041932090426
42744CB00017B/2031